aSTIGMAtism In My Soul!

*A Black American Males adventure
from dead broke to millionaire to
dead broke to white collar crime
incarceration in the United States
Federal Bureau of Prisons (The Feds)
to back on top!*

volume I

DEDICATION

This book is dedicated to me, Sean Xavier Gunby, Sr. I have done what was necessary to complete this undertaking. Through it all – the spiritual and mental wounds, lacerations, contusions, scars and healing, I have seen this Muthaphucka through to the end. Little did I know that those spiritual wars, spiritual battles and "punches in the mouth by life" would be the impetus for me to construct and build this literary work. Wounded badly, fatigued and knocked flat on my ass, but, I NEVER gave up and NEVER will!

This book is dedicated to "My Sun", Sean Xavier Gunby, Jr. The resurrection of myself through birth. It was you that put "wind in my sail" and kept our ship afloat when the waves came crashing over the hull and we were taking on water and things got real funky. When I didn't believe in me.. you did. When I became enveloped in self-hatred and didn't like myself, you told me you loved me under your own volition. When I was weak and lacked courage and strength, you showed me how to be strong. Yeap... it was you that made me keep pushin' and urged me to go on and see what the end was gonna be. You are the love of my life!

This book is dedicated to my mother, Georgia Gunby. Thank you for holding Sean, Jr. down while I was in the joint. Thank you for holding me down while I was in the joint too and from the beginning of my existence on Planet Earth. No matter how bad I've fucked up you have ALWAYS rode wit a Nigga no matter what. I appreciate that! Our story ain't over, we still writing. He who laughs last … laughs best!

SPECIAL DEDICATION

This book is also specially dedicated to the fake family and friends who turned on me when the Feds came. To the fake muthaphucka's who cooperated with the Feds against me. To the clients who begged me to help them (and when I did) and later signed affidavits to testify against me if I took my case to trial. All your names were in my indictment. I know you did it!

To the muthaphucka's whose families I supported and helped with thousands of dollars... thousands of dollars... and you didn't send me $.50 while I was in prison to get me some tuna or peanut butter. You didn't take Lil Sean $3.49 to get him a happy meal or a loaf of bread. You left The Black God for dead, however, I have risen like The Egyptian Phoenix! I always will!

To the weak ass niggas, non-believers, who said "He's done" when the Feds came... Ha ha ... You amuse and entertain me... fooled you Niggas!! I ain't never done! Nothing is impossible for The Black God!

To certain weak niggas at FCI Morgantown I had static with who tried to get me off my square instead of back out here on the street to be The Professional Black Father that I am. I remain Sucka Free Kid!

To the niggas who hate me ... I mean really hate my guts.... LOLOLOLOLOL..... I am especially grateful to you all as you all keep me sharp, precise, on point and make me invincible!!

ABOUT THE AUTHOR

Sean Xavier Gunby, Sr. was born in Passaic, New Jersey and raised in Clifton, New Jersey. He has lived in Atlanta, Georgia, and other towns and cities in North Jersey.

Sean has a Bachelor of Science degree in Accounting from Morris Brown College *(a Historically Black College & University located in Atlanta, GA).*

Sean earned his Masters of Science degree in Financial Management from the New Jersey Institute of Technology in Newark, New Jersey where he graduated Cum Laude.

Sean earned his Ph.D, Doctorate degree in The Feds at Federal Correctional Institution at Morgantown in Morgantown, West Virginia.

Sean is a professional golf caddie.

Sean has worked in the corporate world as a Financial Analyst doing mergers & acquisitions of real estate brokerage companies throughout the United States. As a Financial Analyst, Sean played a major role in the analysis and acquisition of over 100 real estate brokerage companies throughout the United States of America with an annual Sales Volume of over $10 Billion dollars.

Sean has taught as an Adjunct Professor of Pre-Algebra at Passaic County Community College in Paterson, NJ, Bergen County Community College in Paramus, NJ and Essex County College in Newark, NJ.

He was a licensed New Jersey Real Estate Broker and operated a successful realty brokerage, tax preparation and consulting business with over 1,300 clients in 17 different states until he allowed greed to infect his spirit and mind which lead to him being indicted and pleading guilty to getting his clients back bigger refunds than they were entitled to by overstating deductions and credits. These were federal charges and resulted in Sean serving 15 months, 15 days and 19 hours in The United States Federal Bureau of Prisons or "The Feds".

Sean remains an expert real estate investor.

Sean is an experienced stock and options trader and trades his own account.

Today, Sean is a published author and lives in North Jersey, owns and operates a successful window cleaning business and is a Professional Black Father of a Black Sun.

THE IMPETUS FOR WRITING THIS LITERARY DOCUMENT

My writing of this book was cathartic, therapeutic, interesting and ultimately liberating. It freed me and continues to free me. It was a much needed "surgery of the spirit" that needed to take place so that I could move back in the direction of feeling whole. So much had taken place that sparked the mental movement that urged me to write. Mostly though, it was the self-inflicted harm and damage that I had done to myself for so long. The self-destruction and the self-manufactured chaos that I seemed to create as if I was on auto pilot. The self-defeating learned behaviors and thought patterns of childhood, adolescent and young adult years that had caused me to front on me, to diss me, to jerk me, to destroy me and to ultimately kill me if I remained stuck and didn't act to remedy my mind and my spirit.

And that is precisely what I did............

I knew from the beginning of the surgery that a tremendous war had to take place. A knock down fight, a fight to the death, a fight where there could only be 1 survivor when it was all over. Only 1 Nigga could remain breathing. The other nigga had to die. Knowing this didn't fill my mind or my heart with trepidation, anxiety or nervousness. There was absolutely no fear because I had known for years that this needed to go down, however, I just didn't have the courage or the right circumstance to catch this nigga where I wanted him. Well, as always happens, what you put in your mind and what you put your mind to ---- will materialize in the physical form given consistent thoughts and actions toward that aim. I finally ran into the nigga. The timing was impeccable. Nobody was around but me and him. Nobody was there to see it. Just me and him. Didn't have to worry about the police or any bystander breaking up the fight. Nobody was there but me and him. He couldn't run and more importantly...I couldn't run anymore either. We both had to fight and somebody was gonna die.

By the time we met in The Feds in Morgantown, West Virginia I was ready. I was mentally tight, spiritually fit, focused, determined to win and ready to take it there. That nigga knew that I was different. That I had a different look, a higher vibration, a more robust frequency and the look on my grill was what said it all. He tried to use old tactics that had worked for decades of trying to get in my brain and have me go against me, to have me abandon me, to have me blame me, to have me feel shame, to believe that I was less than and unworthy.

That shit did not penetrate my mind nor my soul anymore. His efforts to mentally fuck me up were futile and he saw it. He knew he was in a bad situation and that his time on Planet Earth was coming to an end and that's just what the fuck happened. I was filled with fear and doubt but I said to myself ..."fuck that shit"... and I stepped to that nigga and we got it in. He didn't have a chance. It was a long fight but in the end, I prevailed and came out the victor. While I was giving it to that nigga I made eye contact with him the entire time so that he and I would both know that I was the one who ended his life.

I had done it. At 46 years old, I had killed me a nigga. I assassinated that muthaphucka. He is gone forever never to return. The nigga that I killed... His name was Sean Xavier Gunby. The Nigga that emerged victorious is Sean Xavier Gunby, Sr. A whole new brand new Nigga!

A NOTE FROM THE AUTHOR

I did not have this book proofread or edited by anyone. I did not use "correct" grammar or English at times in this book. I did not go back and fix typos, errors and/or misspellings. You will be able to figure out what I was trying to say. I wrote out the book by hand first and then went back and typed it. What I wrote when I wrote it is exactly how I was feeling or felt and that I how I expressed it.

I am very intelligent and could have very well chosen to do this "correction", "mistake catching", "sugar coating" or "pretty little bow on top" to my document. I decided against same. My reasoning is that this document is "organic" and reality. In our lives we cannot go back and fix, white out, backspace, cut & paste, delete or photoshop our choices and decisions that we make whether those decisions were excellent or fucked up! You can't go backwards…..you can only move forward and live with the choices and decisions that you have made. I chose to do the same with this document.

I am a Soul Writer….. a Soul Author…. I write from my soul and that's as real as real can be.

Hence, I chose to leave this Muthaphucka exactly as I felt it at the time I was writing it. I am not trying to produce a "likable", "appealing to the masses" or "conforming" document. I wrote what the fuck is inside of me. I make real shit because life is real.

What is in the book is exact nature and actual facts.

Thank you

Sean Xavier Gunby, Sr.

LET'S HAVE A PAPERWORK PARTY

Some of you will wonder, hypothesize, conjecture and ramble on about why this is the very first section of my manuscript. Most of you will most likely with a high degree of probability come to a wrong erroneous conclusion as to why.

Others, who are in the know, who know what a "paperwork party" is, will totally understand and know why and there will be no conjecture or imagination needed.

IN THE UNITED STATES DISTRICT COURT
FOR THE DISTRICT OF NEW JERSEY

UNITED STATES OF AMERICA	)	
	)	
vs.	)	PRESENTENCE INVESTIGATION REPORT
	)	
SEAN GUNBY	)	Docket No. 13-00614-001

Prepared For: THE HONORABLE ███████████████
United States District Judge

Prepared By: ███████████
Senior U.S. Probation Officer
Newark, New Jersey 07102
(973) 645-4240

Assistant U.S. Attorney
███████████
970 Broad Street
Room 502
Newark, New Jersey 07102
(973) 645-2700

Defense Counsel
███████████, AFPD
1002 Broad Street
Newark, New Jersey 07102
(973) 645-6347

Sentence Date: 06/04/14

Offense: Count 12: Aiding & Assisting in Preparation of False Income Tax Returns
26 U.S.C. § 7206(2) - 3 years/$250,000, a Class E felony

Arrest Date: 10/03/13

Release Status: 10/03/13: Released on $100,000 unsecured appearance bond

Detainers: None

Codefendants: None

Related Cases: None

Date Report Prepared: 03/31/14   Final Report Prepared: 4/28/14

Identifying Data:

Date of Birth:	03/11/69
Age:	45
Race:	Black or African American, Non-Hispanic origin
Sex:	Male

SSN:	▓▓▓▓▓▓▓
FBI #:	663436JA8
USM #:	65932-050
Other ID #:	NJDL#: ▓▓▓▓▓▓▓▓▓
	NJ SBI#: 511173D
	NY SID#: 6277352Y
	GA State ID#: 1440808W
	Georgia DL#: ▓▓▓▓▓▓
PACTS #:	314182

Education:	Masters Degree
Dependents:	One child
Citizenship:	U.S. Citizen

Legal Address:	57 Gardner Avenue
	Jersey City, NJ 07304

Aliases:	Sean Gundy
	Sean Xavier Gunsby

Offense Level Computation

25. The November 1, 2013, edition of the Guidelines Manual has been used in this case.

Count 12 - Aiding/Assisting Preparation of False Tax Returns

26. **Base Offense Level:** The United States Sentencing Commission Guideline for violation of 26 U.S.C. § 7206(2) is found in U.S.S.G. §§ 2T1.4(a)(1) & 2T4.1(F), which calls for a base offense level of 16, as the tax loss of $84,559 exceeds $80,000 but is less than $200,000.   16

27. **Specific Offense Characteristic:** The defendant was in the business of preparing or assisting in the preparation of tax returns, therefore, two levels are added, pursuant to U.S.S.G. § 2T1.4(b)(1)(B).   +2

28. **Victim-Related Adjustments:** None.   0

29. **Adjustments for Role in the Offense:** None.   0

30. **Adjustment for Obstruction of Justice:** None.   0

31. **Adjusted Offense Level (Subtotal)**   18

32. **Adjustment for Acceptance of Responsibility:** Pursuant to U.S.S.G. § 3E1.1(a), the offense level is reduced two levels.   -2

33. **Additional Adjustment for Acceptance of Responsibility:** Pursuant to U.S.S.G. § 3E1.1(b), the offense level is reduced one additional level provided a motion by the Government is granted at sentencing.   -1

34. **Adjusted Offense Level:**   15

35. **Chapter Four Enhancements:** None.   0

36. **Total Offense Level:**   15

PART B. DEFENDANT'S CRIMINAL HISTORY

Juvenile Adjudication(s)

37. None.

Adult Criminal Conviction(s)

38. NOTE: New Jersey Court Rules 3:4-2(b) and (c) (formerly 3:27-1 and 27-2) require all defendants charged with indictable and non-indictable offenses to be advised by the Court of their right to retain counsel, or if indigent, the right of assigned counsel, in accordance with the Public Defender Act of July 30, 1967.

	Date of Arrest	Conviction/Court	Date Sentence Imposed/Disposition	Guideline	Pnt
39.	12/06/91 (Age: 22)	Abandonment of Certain Dangerous Drugs, Poisons or Controlled Substances & Purchase, Possess, Control Controlled Substances; Fulton County (GA) Superior Court (Dkt#: 990000007643003)	05/28/92: 5 years custody, suspended, to be served on Intensive Probation, drug treatment, $20 monthly probation fee	4A1.2(e)(2)	0
			01/05/1993: VOP Warrant issued		
			02/12/93: VOP Hearing: 8 years probation, w last 30 days of each year to be served in jail for the first 3 years, 200 hours CSW		
			03/04/05: Discharged from probation		

40. While arrest reports were no longer available, all court documentation was provided by Georgia officials. The charging instrument indicates Gunby possessed cocaine with intent to distribute.

Supervision Adjustment

41. Records indicate Gunby was sentenced under the First Offender Act to a probationary term of five years in 1992. He subsequently violated the terms of probation by failing to abide by curfew on eight occasions and failing to pay the monthly fee. His First Offender status was revoked and Gunby was resentenced for to probation for eight years. Special conditions imposed mandated that Gunby serve the last 30 days of each calendar year in jail for the first three years, and also serve 200 hours of community service. Records further show that Gunby was not discharged from probation until March 4, 2005. There was no further information concerning his probation term.

Criminal History Computation

42. The total of the criminal history points is zero. According to the sentencing table at U.S.S.G. Chapter 5, Part A, zero criminal history points establish a criminal history category of I.

Pending Charges

*43. (Deleted).

*44. (Deleted).

Other Arrests

Date of Arrest	Charge	Agency	Disposition
45.	12/31/88 (age: 19)	Criminal Possession of a Weapon, 3rd (Handgun, defaced)	NYPD	No action taken by NY DA's office

46. The defendant was arrested at West 160th Street and Jumel Place by the New York City Police Department, at approximately 1:30 a.m., in possession of a .32 caliber defaced revolver. Records indicate the case was never docketed and further information regarding the disposition of these charges is awaited from the District Attorney's Office.

47.	02/22/88 (age: 18)	Theft by Taking	Fulton County Marshal's Office	None Reported

48. Due to the age of the case, details of the offense were no longer available. According to Georgia authorities, no disposition was recorded.

49. 06/04/90   Criminal Trespass   Atlanta, GA Police   None reported
     (age: 21)   Department

50. Due to the age of the case, details of the offense were no longer available. According to
     Georgia authorities, no disposition was recorded.

51. 03/23/05   Simple Battery,   Lincoln County, GA   Dismissed
     (age: 36) Criminal Damage to   Sheriff's Department
                Property, Obstruct or
                Hinder Person Making
                Emergency Call

52. Records from the Lincoln County Sheriff's Office allege the defendant assaulted Xavier J.
     Gunby by pushing him up against a wall. When Xavier attempted to call 911, the defendant
     broke all three phones in the residence. Formal charges were not pursued in the case and it
     is considered dismissed.

*52a. 01/20/14 Simple Assault   Jersey City, NJ Police   04/17/14:
     (age: 44)   Department   Dismissed

*52b. On January 20, 2014, Gunby and ▓▓▓▓▓▓▓▓▓▓▓▓▓, the mother of his son, were
     involved in an argument on the street in front of Gunby's Jersey City home. The argument
     was due to Gunby objecting to his son being in or playing on the bed of a friend of ▓▓▓▓
     ▓▓▓▓▓▓. During the argument, Gunby is alleged to have grabbed ▓▓▓▓▓▓▓▓▓▓▓▓.
     shoved her against a motor vehicle, and attempted to strangle her by grabbing her around the
     neck. ▓▓▓▓▓▓▓▓▓▓ slapped Gunby in the face, then her older son, age 15, who was in
     the car, intervened and separated the two. ▓▓▓▓▓▓▓▓▓▓ called police. Within minutes,
     Gunby also telephoned police. Responding officers noted they did not observe injuries to
     ▓▓▓▓▓▓▓▓▓▓. Complaints were filed and the charges are pending. Gunby attended
     anger management classes between March 4, 2014 and March 25, 2014, and presented a
     certificate of completion from the Family Success Center of Horizon Health Center. Positive
     Communication Classes.   On April 17, 2014, charges were dismissed in Jersey City
     Municipal Court.

Motor Vehicle

53. Gunby was cited on October 3, 1987, for driving while his license was suspended, in Dekalb
     County, Georgia. Due to the age of the offense, no disposition was available.

Address	Loan Bal.	Monthly Loan Payment &Rental Rate	Net Rental Income	FMV	Equity
57 Gardner Ave., Jersey City, NJ	$390,000	$1,742 (Unpaid)	- 0 -	$187,000	$(203,000)
1615 Mercier Rd., Lincolnton, GA	$42,800	$334 & $550	$216	$109,000	$66,200
168 Watson St., Lincolnton, GA	$54,400	$425 & $500	$75	$104,700	$50,300
3979 Lovelace Rd., Lincolnton, GA	$29,000	$199 & $400	$201	$100,000	$71,000
1118 Huntely Circle, Thomson, GA	$59,800	$467 & $750	$283	$95,600	$35,800
264 Elm Street, Lincolnton, GA	$55,000	$431 & $600	$169	$130,500	$75,500
2333 Metasville Rd., Lincolnton, GA	$51,000	$354 & $450	$96	$130,000	$79,000
2044 Pineywoods Rd., Lincolnton, GA	$40,000	$307 & $501	$194	$123,800	$83,800
110 Max Drive, Washington, GA	$49,000	$335 & $600	$265	$72,300	$23,300
178 Watson St., Lincolnton, GA	$50,000	$413 & $550	$137	$105,000	$55,000
(Blanket Loan)	$103,321	$669	N/A	N/A	N/A
Totals	$873,321	$3,964 & $4,901	$967 ($1,636 - $669 blanket loan)	$1,157,900	$336,900

73. The information provided by Gunby regarding his properties is included in the following profile:

THESE VALUES WERE DELIBERATELY OVERSTATED TO MAKE IT APPEAR THAT I HAD AMPLE FUNDS TO PAY RESTITUTION. THE PROPERTIES WERE WORTH FAR LESS.

- 19 -

RECEIVED

10/31 - Motions
11/14 - Opposition
TBA Hearing
12/5 - Trial

UNITED STATES DISTRICT COURT
DISTRICT OF NEW JERSEY

UNITED STATES OF AMERICA	:	Criminal No. 13-614 (CCC)
v.	:	26 U.S.C. § 7206(2)
SEAN GUNBY	:	INDICTMENT

913 645

The Grand Jury in and for the District of New Jersey, sitting at

Newark, charges:

COUNTS 1-28

1. At all times relevant to this Indictment, defendant SEAN

GUNBY, was a resident of Jersey City, New Jersey, and was self-employed as a

preparer of federal income tax returns.

2. At all times relevant to this Indictment, defendant SEAN GUNBY

was the owner and operator of GUNBY CONSULTING, INC. and GUNBY

CONSULTING GROUP, located in Clifton, New Jersey.

3. At various times relevant to this Indictment, defendant SEAN

GUNBY:

      a. met with individual taxpayers at the office described in

paragraph 2 to prepare their U.S. individual income tax returns;

      b. prepared false U.S. individual income tax returns for his

clients by fabricating and inflating itemized deductions on Schedule A, expenses,

on Schedule C, capital gains and losses on Schedule D, and supplemental

United States District Court
District of New Jersey

In the Matter of the Search of

the business premises of
Sean X. Gunby, d/b/a
GUNBY REALTY,
790 Bloomfield Ave.,
Building A, Suite #4,
Clifton, New Jersey,
As More Particularly
Described in Attachment A

SEARCH WARRANT

Misc. No.11-8042

To: Special Agent ███████████ and any Authorized Officer of the United States

Affidavit having been made before me by Special Agent ███████████ who has reason to believe
that on the premises known as

SEE ATTACHMENT A

in the District of New Jersey there is now concealed a certain person or property, namely

SEE ATTACHMENT B

I am satisfied that the affidavit and any recorded testimony establish probable cause to believe that
the person or property so described is now concealed on the person or premises above-described
and establish grounds for the issuance of this warrant.

YOU ARE HEREBY COMMANDED to execute this warrant on or before __April 27, 2011__
                                                                    Date (not to exceed 14 days)
on the person or place named above for the person or property specified, serving this warrant and
making the search in the daytime, 6:00 a.m. to 10:00 p.m., and if the person or property be found
there to seize same, leaving a copy of this warrant and receipt for the person or property taken, and
prepare a written inventory of the person or property seized and promptly return this warrant to the
Honorable ███████████ U.S. Magistrate Judge as required by law.

April 13, 2011,   at   Newark, New Jersey
Date and Time Issued   City and State

Honorable ███████████
United States Magistrate Judge
Name and Title of Judicial Officer   Signature of Judicial Officer

Inventory Listing of All Items Seized at Search Warrant Site

Site Name:	Investigation Number:	Report Date:
790 Bloomfield Avenue, Suite 4	1000238624	Thursday, April 14, 2011
Clifton, NJ 07012	Starting Date and Time:	
Office of Sean X. Gunby	04/14/2011 09:20 AM	
	Ending Date and Time:	
	04/14/2011 11:15 AM	

Control #:	1	Evidence Box:	1
Location:	SECRETARY'S OFFICE	Locator Code:	B2
Found:	DESK ON LEFT		
Description:	Seized Per Warrant	CLIENT TAX RETURN DOCS, 2 MESSAGE BOOKS	

Control #:	2	Evidence Box:	2
Location:	SECRETARY'S OFFICE	Locator Code:	B3
Found:	FILING CABINET		
Description:	Seized Per Warrant	GUNBY REALTY FOLDERS 2006-2010	

Control #:	3	Evidence Box:	3
Location:	SECRETARY'S OFFICE	Locator Code:	B3
Found:	FILING CABINET		
Description:	Seized Per Warrant	GUNBY REALTY FOLDERS, CLIENT EFILE FORMS & 2 PAYROLL BINDERS	

Control #:	4	Evidence Box:	4
Location:	SECRETARY'S OFFICE	Locator Code:	B3
Found:	FILING CABINET		
Description:	Seized Per Warrant	GUNBY REALTY FOLDERS AND MISC TAX DOCUMENTS	

Control #:	5	Evidence Box:	1
Location:	SECRETARY'S OFFICE	Locator Code:	B4
Found:	DESK ON RIGHT		
Description:	Seized Per Warrant	PHONE MESSAGE BOOKS (12), FORMS 8879, INDEMNITY BOND, DAY MINDERS 2008, 2009, 2010 , GUNBY CONSULTING-CHECK PICKUP-SIGN IN SHEETS (4)	

Control #:	6	Evidence Box:	5
Location:	GUNBY'S OFFICE	Locator Code:	A2
Found:	TABLE		
Description:	Seized Per Warrant	2007-2010 CLIENT TAX RETURNS & SUPPORTING DOCS AND 1 BAG CONTAINING TAX PREP DOCUMENTS	

Control #:	7	Evidence Box:	6
Location:	GUNBY'S OFFICE	Locator Code:	A4
Found:	FILING CABINET		
Description:	Seized Per Warrant VARIOUS FINANCIAL DOCUMENTS INCLUDING BANK DOCUMENTS AND TAX RETURNS		

Control #:	8	Evidence Box:	6
Location:	GUNBY'S OFFICE	Locator Code:	A4
Found:	R. SIDE OF FILING CABINET ON FLOOR		
Description:	Seized Per Warrant TAX PREPARATION INFORMATION		

Control #:	9	Evidence Box:	7
Location:	GUNBY'S OFFICE	Locator Code:	A3
Found:	DRAWERS & ON TOP OF DESK		
Description:	Seized Per Warrant FINANCIAL AND MISCELLANEOUS DOCUMENTS		

Control #:	10	Evidence Box:	8
Location:	GUNBY'S OFFICE	Locator Code:	A1
Found:	SHELVES AGAINST LEFT WALL		
Description:	Seized Per Warrant VARIOUS IRS RELATED DOCUMENTS AND FINANCIAL RECORDS		

Control #:	11	Evidence Box:	8
Location:	GUNBY'S OFFICE	Locator Code:	A1
Found:	SHELVES AGAINST LEFT WALL		
Description:	Seized Per Warrant VARIOUS IRS RELATED DOCUMENTS AND FINANCIAL RECORDS		

Control #:	12	Evidence Box:	
Location:	SECRETARY'S OFFICE	Locator Code:	B4
Found:	DESK ON RIGHT		
Description:	Seized Per Warrant IMAGE OF DELL DESKTOP S/N 7FQCHH1		

Control #:	13	Evidence Box:	
Location:	GUNBY'S OFFICE	Locator Code:	A3
Found:	DESK		
Description:	Seized Per Warrant IMAGE OF DELL DESKTOP S/N G9Y9HB1		

Control #:	14	Evidence Box:	
Location:	SECRETARY'S OFFICE	Locator Code:	B2
Found:	DESK ON LEFT		
Description:	Seized Per Warrant IMAGE OF DELL DESKTOP S/N G130521		

UNITED STATES DISTRICT COURT
District of New Jersey

REC~ ~~

AUG 1 3 2~~

U.S. PROBAT~~
NEWAR~, ~

UNITED STATES OF AMERICA

v.

SEAN GUNBY

Defendant.

Case Number   2:13-CR-614 (CCC)

JUDGMENT IN A CRIMINAL CASE
(For Offenses Committed On or After November 1, 1987)

The defendant, SEAN GUNBY, was represented by

The defendant pled guilty to count(s) 1 of the INDICTMENT on December 16, 2013. Accordingly, the court has adjudicated that the defendant is guilty of the following offense(s):

Title & Section	Nature of Offense	Date of Offense	Count Number(s)
26:7206(2)	AIDING & ASSISTING IN THE PREPARATION OF FALSE TAX RETURNS	2/21/08-5/3/11	1

As pronounced on August 6, 2014, the defendant is sentenced as provided in pages 2 through 6 of this Judgment. The sentence is imposed pursuant to the Sentencing Reform Act of 1984.

It is ordered that the defendant shall pay to the United States a special assessment of $100, for count(s) 1, which shall be due immediately. Said special assessment shall be made payable to the Clerk, U.S. District Court.

It is further ordered that the defendant shall notify the United States Attorney for this district within 30 days of any change of name, residence, or mailing address until all fines, restitution, costs, and special assessments imposed by this Judgment are fully paid. If ordered to pay restitution, the defendant shall notify the court and United States Attorney of any material change in the defendant's economic circumstances.

Signed this the _8_ day of August, 2014.

I HEREBY CERTIFY that the above and foregoing is a true and correct copy of the original on file in my office.
ATTEST
_____, Clerk
United States District Court
District of New Jersey

By:_____
Deputy Clerk

_____
United States District Judge

07304

WILFREDO TORRES
CHIEF PROBATION OFFICER

THOMAS C. MILLER
SR. DEPUTY CHIEF PROBATION OFFICER

BETH L. NEUGASS
DEPUTY CHIEF PROBATION OFFICER

August 26, 2014

U.S. COURTHOUSE
50 WALNUT STREET
ROOM 1001
NEWARK, NJ 07102
(973) 645-4240
FAX: (973) 645-3173

www.njp.uscourts.gov

Sean Gunby
57 Gardner Avenue
Jersey City, NJ 07304

Reg. Number: 65932-050
DOB: 03/11/1969
Docket Number: 13-00614-001
PACTS Number: 314182

Re: VOLUNTARY SURRENDER TO DESIGNATED INSTITUTION

Dear Mr. Gunby:

This is to inform you that the Federal Bureau of Prisons has designated Federal Correctional Institution located at Morgantown, 446 Greenbag Road, Route 857, Morgantown, WV 26501 as the institution for you to serve your sentence.

You are to voluntarily surrender to this institution at or before NOON on Monday, October 6, 2014. If you have any specific questions concerning the facility, please call the institution directly at 304-296-4416.

Please understand that your failure to comply with this order will result in the institution considering you to be a fugitive.

Very truly yours,

Administrative Assistant

mw

cc: The Honorable ████████, USDJ
    AUSA ████████
    AFPD ████████
    U.S. Marshal, Newark, N.J.
    Pretrial Services, D/NJ
    Institution
    File

INMATE SKILLS DEVELOPMENT PLAN

Current Program Review: 12-09-2015

Identification

Name:		
Register Number:		
Age/Sex/Race:		
Proposed Release:		

Inmate Information

Telephone

Substance Region

16-06-2016

INMATE SKILLS DEVELOPMENT PLAN

PROGRAM REVIEW: 12-09-2015

Special Conditions of Supervision

Profile Comments:

EDUCATION DATA

Facility	Assignment	Start Date	Stop Date
MRC	ESL HAS		CURRENT
MRC	GED HAS		CURRENT
MRC	MAIN (HIGH)		CURRENT

COMPLETED EDUCATION COURSES

Course Description	Completion Date	Current Hours

COMPLETED EDUCATION COURSES

HIGHEST PROGRAM

Test	Subtest	Score	Test Date	Form

WORK DATA

Facility	Assignment	Start Date	Stop Date

Jersey City man sentenced to 18 months for preparing fraudulent tax returns

By **Michaelangelo Conte | The Jersey Journal**
Follow on Twitter
on August 19, 2014 at 4:38 PM, updated August 19, 2014 at 4:57 PM

A Jersey City man was sentenced to 18 months in prison for preparing fraudulent tax returns in order to obtain larger refunds for his clients, according to court records.

Sean Gunby Sr., 44, is to surrender to the Federal Bureau of Prisons on Oct. 6, officials said in court papers.

Sean Gunby Sr., 44, the sole owner and operator of Gunby Consulting in Clifton, pleaded guilty on Dec. 16 to one count of a 28-count indictment that charged him with aiding and assisting in the preparation of false tax returns, officials said.

As part of the Aug. 6 sentence meted out by U.S. District Court Judge Claire C. Cecchi, Gunby must repay more than $84,000 and upon his release from prison he must "refrain from working, directly or indirectly, as a tax preparer or for a tax preparation business."

"While most return preparers provide excellent service to their clients, a few dishonest tax preparers file false and fraudulent returns to defraud the government, the taxpaying public and their own clients," Shantelle P. Kitchen, Special Agent in Charge, IRS-Criminal Investigation, Newark Field Office said in a statement said at the time of Gunby's guilty plea.

Kitchen continued saying that " ... the taxpaying public can be assured that IRS-Criminal Investigation will continue to vigilantly identify and investigate fraudulent preparers like Mr. Gunby."

Gunby admitted that from 2006 through 2010 he prepared false personal tax returns for his clients by fabricating and inflating certain expenses, deductions and credits.

That allowed Gunby to obtain tax refunds for his clients greater than what they were lawfully entitled to. The total amount of tax defrauded was about $84,559, officials said.

WILFREDO TORRES
CHIEF PROBATION OFFICER

BETH L. NEUGASS
SR. DEPUTY CHIEF PROBATION OFFICER

MAUREEN KELLY
DEPUTY CHIEF PROBATION OFFICER

SUSAN M. SMALLEY
DEPUTY CHIEF PROBATION OFFICER

UNITED STATES DISTRICT COURT
PROBATION OFFICE
DISTRICT OF NEW JERSEY

March 10, 2017

U.S. COURTHOUSE
50 WALNUT ST.
ROOM 1001
NEWARK, NJ 07102
(973) 645-6161
FAX: (973) 645-2155

www.njp.uscourts.gov

Sean Gunby
249 Belleville Avenue
Apartment 47B
Bloomfield, NJ 07003

Re: Termination of Supervision

Dear Mr. Gunby:

On January 21, 2017, your term of supervised release obligation expired. You no longer have any obligations to this office.

We hope you benefited from the period of supervision and wish you success in the future. Do not hesitate to contact this office if you have any questions.

Very truly yours,

WILFREDO TORRES, Chief
U.S. Probation Officer

U.S. Probation Officer

/jhr

October 8, 2017

Mr. Sean Xavier Gunby, Sr.
249 Belleville Ave #47B
Bloomfield, New Jersey 07003

RE: UNIVERSAL PARDON

Mr. Gunby, Sr.,

We have carefully observed, examined and witnessed your spiritual, mental and physical transmutation and all of the requisite changes you made to your core self, resulting in your meteoric vibration expansion. You have done what was necessary and we are pleased with your results.

Your rights, in every facet of the word, are hereby solidified and restored. Your rights have been endowed and augmented with a Universal robustness only bequeathed to those who are true to themselves and to The Universe. We are pleased that you accept and have shown your humanness and that you admit and accept your shortcomings and errors. This we love. You exemplify and embody the qualities of tenacity, manhood, determination, perseverance, spirit, courage, strength, love and compassion. This we love.

We hereby decree with all of the ethereal space, vibration, energy, spirit and frequencies of the Cosmos of which we are THE ALL, that you are hereby pardoned for any of your past transgressions, errors in judgment and mistakes, because to us, The Universe, these are only "life experiences" and "school" to which every human being will matriculate through.

Always remember, *"Everything that's inside the Universe is inside of you"*

Congratulations Mr. Gunby, we love you now and always will until infinity. We give you permission to sign your own pardon on your own behalf. Stay strong Black Man.

Supremely, Majestically, Universally

The Sun, The Moon and The Stars

10/8/17

TD Ameritrade
Member FINRA/SIPC/NFA

SEANGUNDY
790 BLOOMFIELD AVE
STE 4
CLIFTON, NJ 07012-1143

2011 Consolidated Forms 1099

Tax Identification Number:
Account Number:

TD AMERITRADE
DIVISION OF TD AMERITRADE INC
PO BOX 2209
OMAHA, NE 68103-2209

For 1099 questions, please call:
800-669-3900

TD Ameritrade Clearing, Inc., Federal Tax Identification Number: 47-0933629

This is important tax information and is being furnished to the Internal Revenue Service. If you are required to file a return, a negligence penalty or other sanction may be imposed on you if this income is taxable and the IRS determines that it has not been reported.

Form 1099-DIV Dividends and Distributions	(OMB No: 1545-0110)	
Line #	Category	Amount
1a	Total Ordinary Dividends	$290.01
1b	Qualified Dividends	290.01
2a	Total Capital Gains Distributions (includes Lines 2b, 2c, 2d)	0.00
2b	Unrecaptured Section 1250 Gain	0.00
2c	Section 1202 Gain	0.00
2d	Collectibles (28%) Gain	0.00
3	Nontaxable Distributions	0.00
4	Federal Income Tax Withheld	0.00
5	Investment Expenses	0.00
6	Foreign Tax Paid	0.00
7	Foreign Country or U.S. Possession	See Details
8	Liquidation Distribution - Cash	0.00
9	Liquidation Distribution - Noncash	0.00

Form 1099-B Proceeds From Broker & Barter Exchange Transactions	(OMB No: 1545-0715)	
Line #	Category	Amount
1a	Date of Sale or Exchange	See Details
1b	Date of Acquisition	See Details
2	Stocks, Bonds, Etc Reported To IRS	
	- Gross Proceeds Less Commissions and Options Premiums	5,757,338.69
3	Cost or Other Basis	1,855,705.82
4	Federal Income Tax Withheld	0.00
5	Wash Sale Loss Disallowed	137,692.80
6	Covered or Uncovered Security	See Details
8	Type of Gain or Loss	See Details
9	Description	See Details
	REGULATED FUTURES CONTRACTS	
10	Profit or (loss) realized in 2011 on closed contracts	0.00
11	Unrealized profit or (loss) on open contracts - 12/31/2010	0.00
12	Unrealized profit or (loss) on open contracts - 12/31/2011	0.00
13	Aggregate profit or (loss) on contracts	0.00
14	Bartering	.

02/06/12

TD Ameritrade	**Tax Information**	Statement Date: 02/07/2013	**2012**
Ameritrade.com	▬▬▬▬	Document ID: ▬▬▬▬	

| PO BOX 2209
OMAHA, NE 68103-2209
Customer Service: 800-669-3900 | SEAN GUNBY
57 GARDNER AVE
JERSEY CITY, NJ 07304-3013 | x | |

PAYER'S Federal ID No: 47-0533629   RECIPIENT'S ID No ▬▬▬▬

Dividends and Distributions

	2012 1099-DIV* OMB No. 1545-0110
1a- Total ordinary dividends (includes line 1b)	255.89
1b- Qualified dividends	255.89
2a- Total capital gain distributions (includes lines 2b, 2c, 2d)	0.00
2b- Unrecaptured section 1250 gain	0.00
2c- Section 1202 gain	0.00
2d- Collectibles (28%) gain	0.00
3- Nondividend distributions	0.00
4- Federal income tax withheld	0.00
5- Investment expenses	0.00
6- Foreign tax paid	0.00
7- Foreign country or US possession	
8- Cash liquidation distributions	0.00
9- Noncash liquidation distributions	0.00
10- Exempt-interest dividends (includes line 11)	0.00
11- Specified private activity bond interest dividends (AMT)	0.00
12- State 13- State ID number	
14- State tax withheld	0.00

Interest Income

	2012 1099-INT* OMB No. 1545-0112
1- Interest income (not included in line 3)	4.34
2- Early withdrawal penalty	0.00
3- Interest on US Savings Bonds & Treasury obligations	0.00
4- Federal income tax withheld	0.00
5- Investment expenses	0.00
6- Foreign tax paid	0.00
7- Foreign country or US possession	
8- Tax-exempt interest (includes line 9)	0.00
9- Specified private activity bond interest (AMT)	0.00
10- Tax-exempt bond CUSIP number (see instructions)	
11- State 12- State ID number	
13- State tax withheld	0.00

Lines 8 & 9 include tax-exempt interest and original issue discount. Exempt-interest dividends from mutual funds now appear on the 1099-DIV.

Regulated Futures Contracts

	2012 1099-B* OMB No. 1545-0215
8- Profit (loss) realized in 2012 closed contracts	0.00
9- Unrealized profit (loss) open contracts 12/31/2011	0.00
10- Unrealized profit (loss) open contracts 12/31/2012	0.00
11- Aggregate profit (loss) on contracts	0.00

Miscellaneous Income

	2012 1099-MISC* OMB No. 1545-0115
2- Royalties	0.00
3- Other income	0.00
4- Federal income tax withheld	0.00
8- Substitute payments in lieu of dividends or interest	0.00
16- State tax withheld	0.00
17- State Payer's state ID number	
18- State income	0.00

* This is important tax information and is being furnished to the Internal Revenue Service. If you are required to file a return, a negligence penalty or other sanction may be imposed on you if this income is taxable and the IRS determines that it has not been reported.

SUMMARY OF GROSS PROCEEDS AND ORIGINAL ISSUE DISCOUNT

The will report the informational totals shown below as your tax return. Use details from the Forms 1099-B and 1099-OID on the following pages to determine reportable amounts.

Gross Proceeds Summary

Gross proceeds less commissions	7,616,126.70
Federal income tax withheld	0.00

Original Issue Discount Summary

Original issue discount for 2012	0.00
Other periodic interest	0.00
Federal income tax withheld	0.00
Original issue Discount on US Treasury Obligations	0.00
Investment expenses	0.00

Changes to dividend tax classifications processed after your original tax form is issued for 2012 may require an amended form 1099.

TD AMERITRADE CLEARING INC

Supplemental Information

Account

2012

SUMMARY OF GAINS AND LOSSES

These amounts are for informational purposes. Cost basis totals only amounts that were available to us. Any amounts shown with an undetermined term must be reviewed to establish whether the gains losses are short-term or long-term. Refer to the appropriate detail schedule on the following pages to review that you consider all relevant items and to determine if the cost basis figures are correct for your tax return.

Term Category	Detail Schedule		Proceeds	Cost Basis	Wash Sale Loss Disallowed	Net Capital Gain/Loss
Short						
A (basis reported to the IRS)	Form 1099-B		7,071,945.10	7,247,343.96	120,951.09	-176,298.75
Long						
A (basis reported to the IRS)	Form 1099-B		107,992.23	142,349.57	0.00	-34,566.34
B (basis not reported to the IRS)	Form 1099-B		498,441.46	0.00	0.00	0.00
		Total	544,483.69	142,990.57	0.00	-34,566.34

SUMMARY OF NON REPORTED INCOME, FEES, EXPENSES AND EXPENDITURES

The items in this section are not reported to the IRS. They are presented here for your reference when preparing your tax return.

Interest Payments and Other Adjustments

Taxable accrued interest paid	0.00
Tax-exempt accrued interest paid	0.00
Tax-exempt accrued interest paid AMT	0.00
Taxable accrued interest paid on OID bonds	0.00
Non-qualified interest	0.00
Taxable non-qualified interest paid	0.00
Projected interest shortfall on contingent payment debt	0.00

Other Receipts

Partnership distributions	0.00
Foreign tax paid - partnership distributions	0.00
Return of principal distributions	0.00
Deferred income payment	0.00

Expenses

Margin interest	6,596.27
Dividends paid - short position	416.32
Interest paid - short position	0.00
Non reportable distribution expense	0.00
Other expenses	0.00
Severance tax	0.00

Opening Transactions

Securities purchased	3,216,285.53
Installment payments	0.00
Short sales	-3,653,149.72

Fees and Payments Received

Deemed premium	0.00
Organizational expense	0.00
Income accrual - UIT	0.00
Miscellaneous fees	0.00
Basis adjustments	0.00
Tax-exempt investment expense	0.00

Options Transactions

Sales	12,978,491.73
Short sales	15,703.85
Purchases	0.00
Purchases to close	34,543.77

| **TD Ameritrade** | **Tax Information** Account ••••••• | Statement Date: 01/18/2014 Document ID: ••••••••• | **2013** |

PO BOX 2209
OMAHA, NE 68103-2209
Customer Service: 800-669-3900

SEAN GUMBY
97 GARDNER AVE
JERSEY CITY, NJ 07304-3013

PAYER'S Federal ID No: 47-0533629   RECIPIENT'S ID No ••••••••

Dividends and Distributions — 2013 1099-DIV* OMB No. 1545-0110

1a- Total ordinary dividends (includes line 1b)	0.00
1b- Qualified dividends	0.00
2a- Total capital gain distributions (includes lines 2b, 2c, 2d)	0.00
2b- Unrecaptured Section 1250 gain	0.00
2c- Section 1202 gain	0.00
2d- Collectibles (28%) gain	0.00
3- Nondividend distributions	0.00
4- Federal income tax withheld	0.00
5- Investment expenses	0.00
7- Foreign country or US possession 9- Foreign tax paid	0.00
8- Cash liquidation distributions	0.00
9- Noncash liquidation distributions	0.00
10- Exempt-interest dividends (includes line 11)	0.00
11- Specified private activity bond interest dividends (AMT)	0.00
12- State 13- State ID number	
14- State tax withheld	0.00

Interest Income — 2013 1099-INT* OMB No. 1545-0112

1- Interest income (not included in line 3)	1.03
2- Early withdrawal penalty	0.00
3- Interest on US Savings Bonds & Treasury obligations	0.00
4- Federal income tax withheld	0.00
5- Investment expenses	0.00
7- Foreign country or US possession: 8- Foreign tax paid	0.00
6- Tax-exempt interest (includes line 9)	0.00
9- Specified private activity bond interest (AMT)	0.00
10- Tax-exempt bond CUSIP number (see instructions)	
11- State 12- State ID number	
13- State tax withheld	0.00

Lines 8 & 9 include tax-exempt interest and original issue discount

Regulated Futures Contracts — 2013 1099-B* OMB No. 1545-0715

9- Profit (loss) realized in 2013 closed contracts	0.00
10- Unrealized profit (loss) open contracts 12/31/2012	0.00
11- Unrealized profit (loss) open contracts 12/31/2013	0.00
12- Aggregate profit (loss) on contracts	0.00

If applicable, summaries and details of proceeds from sale transactions appear in subsequent sections of this document.

Miscellaneous Income — 2013 1099-MISC* OMB No. 1545-0115

2- Royalties	0.00
3- Other income	0.00
4- Federal income tax withheld	0.00
8- Substitute payments in lieu of dividends or interest	0.00
12- Foreign country or US possession 11- Foreign tax paid	0.00
16- State tax withheld	0.00
17- State Payer's state ID number	
18- State income	0.00

* This is important tax information and is being furnished to the Internal Revenue Service. If you are required to file a return, a negligence penalty or other sanction may be imposed on you if this income is taxable and the IRS determines that it has not been reported.

ORIGINAL ISSUE DISCOUNT SUMMARY

Use these to complete the 1099-OID steps to determine reportable amounts of Original Issue Discount income for your tax returns. The informational totals shown below appear for reference only.

Original issue discount for 2013	0.00	Original issue discount on US Treasury obligations	0.00
Other periodic interest	0.00	Investment expenses	0.00
Early withdrawal penalty	0.00	State State ID number	
Federal income tax withheld	0.00	State tax withheld	0.00
Foreign country or US possession Foreign tax paid	0.00		

Changes in dividend tax classifications processed after your original tax form is issued for 2013 may require an amended form 1099.

TD Ameritrade	Tax Information	Statement Date: 01/27/2016	**2014**
	Account [redacted]	Document ID: [redacted]	

PO BOX 2209
OMAHA, NE 68103-2209
Customer Service: 800-669-3900

SEAN GUNBY
3694 LOVELACE RD
LINCOLNTON, GA 30817-3256

PAYER'S Federal ID No: 47-0533629   RECIPIENT'S ID No: [redacted]

Summary Information

DIVIDENDS AND DISTRIBUTIONS   2014 1099-DIV*   (OMB No. 1545-0110)

1a- Total ordinary dividends (includes line 1b)	0.00
1b- Qualified dividends	0.00
2a- Total capital gain distributions (includes lines 2b, 2c, 2d)	0.00
2b- Unrecaptured Section 1250 gain	0.00
2c- Section 1202 gain	0.00
2d- Collectibles (28%) gain	0.00
3- Nondividend distributions	0.00
4- Federal income tax withheld	0.00
5- Investment expenses	0.00
7- Foreign country or US possession 6- Foreign tax paid	0.00
8- Cash liquidation distributions	0.00
9- Noncash liquidation distributions	0.00
10- Exempt-interest dividends (includes line 11)	0.00
11- Specified private activity bond interest dividends (AMT)	0.00

MISCELLANEOUS INCOME   2014 1099-MISC*   (OMB No. 1545-0115)

2- Royalties	0.00
3- Other income	0.00
4- Federal income tax withheld	0.00
8- Substitute payments in lieu of dividends or interest	0.00

REGULATED FUTURES CONTRACTS 2014 1099-B*   (OMB No. 1545-0215)

8- Profit or (loss) realized in 2014 on closed contracts	-994.18
9- Unrealized profit or (loss) on open contracts-12/31/2013	0.00
10- Unrealized profit or (loss) on open contracts-12/31/2014	0.00
11- Aggregate profit or (loss) on contracts	-994.18

If applicable, summaries and details of proceeds from sale transactions appear in subsequent sections of this document.

* This is important tax information and is being furnished to the Internal Revenue Service. If you are required to file a return, a negligence penalty or other sanction may be imposed on you if this income is taxable and the IRS determines that it has not been reported.

SALES TRANSACTIONS

Proceeds, gains, losses and adjustments

Refer to the 1099-B and Proceeds not reported to the IRS pages to ensure that you consider all relevant facts and to determine the correct gains and losses. The amounts shown below are for informational purposes.

Term	Form 8949 type	Proceeds	Cost basis	Market discount	Wash sale loss disallowed	Net gain or loss(-)
Short	A (basis reported to the IRS)	555,588.23	617,272.34	0.00	20,996.98	-40,687.13
Short	B (basis not reported to the IRS)	0.00	0.00	0.00	0.00	0.00
Short	C (Form 1099-B not received)	0.00	0.00	0.00	0.00	0.00
	Total Short-term	555,588.23	617,272.34	0.00	20,995.98	-40,687.13
Long	D (basis reported to the IRS)	0.00	0.00	0.00	0.00	0.00
Long	E (basis not reported to the IRS)	0.00	0.00	0.00	0.00	0.00
Long	F (Form 1099-B not received)	0.00	0.00	0.00	0.00	0.00
	Total Long-term	0.00	0.00	0.00	0.00	0.00
Undetermined	B or E (basis not reported to the IRS)	0.00	0.00	0.00	0.00	0.00
Undetermined	C or F (Form 1099-B not received)	0.00	0.00	0.00	0.00	0.00
	Total Undetermined-term	0.00	0.00	0.00	0.00	0.00
	Grand total	**555,588.23**	**617,272.34**	**0.00**	**20,995.98**	**-40,687.13**

Withholding from Proceeds

Federal income tax withheld   0.00

Changes to dividend tax classifications processed after your original tax form is issued for 2014 may require an amended tax form.

Morris Brown College

Member of the Atlanta University Center

Atlanta, Georgia

By the authority of the Board of Trustees of Morris Brown College
and upon the recommendation of the Faculty thereof the degree of

Bachelor of Science in Accounting

has been conferred upon

Sean Xavier Guuby

with all the rights and privileges thereunto appertaining.
In Witness Thereof this diploma duly signed has been issued and
the seal of the College attained.

New Jersey Institute of Technology

*The Board of Trustees of New Jersey Institute of Technology, upon recommendation of the Faculty
and in recognition of completion of the requisite course of study, hereby confers upon*

SEAN XAVIER GUNBY

the degree of

MASTER OF SCIENCE IN
MANAGEMENT

with all the rights and privileges thereunto appertaining.

Given under the seal of the University this twenty-third day of May, nineteen hundred and ninety-seven.

Monday, June 20, 2016

I've done it! I've accomplished another goal. 'Cause that's what the fuck I do – accomplish goals. I'mma goal accomplishin' muthaphucka too baby. I guess one would want to know – "what new goal did I accomplish?". Well, about 3 weeks ago I had heard that a dude I have known for 24 plus years was sick and in the hospital. So I bolted over to the hospital to see about my man and when I walked into his room he spoke and said " Brutha Sean!!"... we exchanged greetings and then almost immediately after this exchange he asked me "Have you published anything yet?"

From that moment, that very instant, I made the decision to write and to publish some type of literary work. I have been told to and many, many suggestions have been made to me to write a book. Well today, I started writing and this was a goal I set 3 weeks ago. So I accomplished another goal, which I have repeatedly done for the 47 years I've been on this planet Earth as a Black American Male. I'mma bad muthaphucka!

Tuesday, June 21, 2016 – 4:14pm

There is no doubt whatsoever in my mind that I can accomplish anything I desire. All I have to do is think it, visualize it, and then move on it. I feel tremendous confidence in myself. Ahhhh man!! My best days are in front of me. There is absolutely nothing I can't do – Nothing is impossible for me! I mean nothing!

Later that same day – 9:16pm

To be a Black American Male Father of a Black American Male Sun is the most important role on the Planet Earth – in my opinion. Perhaps I feel this way because I am and have been. I don't know, but I don't believe a Philipino Male, Scandinavian Male or Angolan Male would share my sentiments or thoughts on this matter.

To me, in my opinion and my experience, here in the United States of America, it is imperative that the Black Male Father command and play an active role in the lives of his posterity, especially and more so in the little Black American Male boys. This is of utmost importance, and, in my opinion, there are no excuses. My reasoning is that each little part and leadership role that's played individually, augments, fortifies, strengthens and propels the entire Black American Nation forward and upward. There is absolutely no doubt about this.

And guess what??

The decision lies within each Black American Male Father completely. It is his duty to The Sun, Moon and Stars. The very instant that the Black American Male Father is chosen and bestowed with the Universe's gift of a Black American Male child, he immediately incurs a balance with the "Universe Credit Card". This credit card has and unlimited balance and must be paid in full – down to zero – everyday (23 hours 56 minutes 4 seconds – this is the true length of the "stellar day" or 86,400 seconds).

Payment is made by being an active participant, guide, teacher and leader in the life of your posterity. If counterfeit payments or no payments at all are made after each 86,400 seconds period of time – the balance on the Black American Male Fathers "Universe Credit Card" quadruples and the interest rate on that balance soars astronomically. The Universe then offers no assistance, no rhythm, no vibration and holds the Black American Male Father in contempt of the Cosmos.

Conversely, if that Black American Male Father makes timely and full payments at the end of each "stellar day" – then that Black American Male Father 's magnetism is increased, his frequency and vibration are elevated and everything he needs comes to him with precision, accuracy and automatically……without fail! UNIVERSAL LAW!

From that moment, that very instant, I made the decision to write and to publish some type of literary work. I have been told to and many, many suggestions have been made to me to write a book. Well today, I started writing and this was a goal I set 3 weeks ago. So I accomplished another goal, which I have repeatedly done for the 47 years I've been on this planet Earth as a Black American Male. I'mma bad muthaphucka!

Thursday, June 23, 2016

There is a certain inherent elemental fiber of and inside of every human being (perhaps in every living organism) of which socio-economic status, caste, class, race, nepotism, who you know or what family you are born into – has no influence or bearing. If you are mentally weak and cowardly, you will be this and live and experience all of the psychological discomforts and pains that come with and are a result of this debility.

Conversely, if one is stout-hearted, brave and imbued with fight, you will be this and live and experience all of the psychological pleasures and felicity that comes with this mind set.

Whether you live on Central Park West or you share a cardboard refrigerator box inside the Port Authority of NY/NJ, - this elemental fiber will determine your inner condition and make or mar your happiness. No amount of money or net worth can alter this determination. No familial or social relationship(s) with a senator, judge, or elected official can alter or change this inner condition. A 30 year plus prison sentence or the eating out of the dumpster behind KFC can alter this inner world. Your inner world is made, constructed, fortified, built up and solidified by no thing, person, place other than YOU!

Conversely, your inner world cannot be weakened, demolished, imploded or destroyed by no thing, person or place. Your inner world can only be fucked up and decimated by YOU! This very also applied to me!

I draw this conclusion as a result of my own 47 years of life experience, study and observation. And once again – this is my opinion.

Friday, July 1, 2016

Got me and My Sun a 2BR apartment on Tuesday of this week. Spent the last 3 days moving all of my personal effects from another location to here. It's been an interesting past 72 hours.

This is my 1st place – home of my own in the past 21 months. For the past 5 months, I and My Sun have been living with a supremely good female friend of mine in her basement. For 16 months prior to that I was in "The Feds" – Federal Prison – FCI Morgantown, in Morgantown, West Virginia, serving an 18 month sentence. So it feels awkward as a muthaphucka to be in my own spot with My Sun – but this is also what I planned and envisioned while I was in the joint. It's what motivated me to make the time "serve me" instead of me "serving the time".

I don't have gainful employment or any source of income. For the past 2 months I have been playing poker at the casino for a living and it's been working.

I applied for a job with a private equity firm in Manhattan owned by a colleague I'd worked with in the past. Applied for work at Golds Gym (where I was a member) in Jersey City for $9 per hour, re-racking the weights. Wendy's for $8.75/hr in Roselle, NJ, caddy job at Upper Montclair Country Club, Echo Lake, Arcola Country Club and Baltusrol Country Club. Nothing, nothing, nothing, nothing.

I have a BS degree in Accounting. I also have a MS degree in Financial Management. When you tell muthaphucka's you just got released from "The Feds", muthaphucka's run and hide, scatter and don't want nothing to do with you (most not all).

But there is absolutely no way possible that I will crumble and fold my tent. Ain't no muthaphuckin' way I will quit, give up and let America put out my spirit light, take my self-confidence and make me internalize and believe that I can't make it. Nah!!! Not this Nigga!! I know I'mma bad muthaphucka and I will rise again just as the Phoenix flies!

Sunday, July 3, 2016

It's a real interesting time in my life. I am settling in to a 2BR apartment for me and My Sun. I put down over $3,000 cash between security deposit and 1st months rent and having lost $2,700 playing poker over the past 2 weeks I now have about $112.42 to my name with no prospect of any kind of income coming in.

What do I do?

Get a job making $10 per hour or go back to the casino and play better poker? I don't know. Neither option sounds good but playing better poker is more appealing, more profitable and can get me to where I'm going faster. I know why I lost the last 2 weeks. The "fear of losing" thoughts about "what's going to happen if I lose?", "I can't lose" instead of "what' I'm going to buy for my new apartment when I win", "when I win today" – thoughts about winning big pots. That's where my mind is supposed to be. On winning – on success – on achieving my daily poker goal – on winning that day. Thoughts like that are more conducive to success than the fear of failing. I ain't gonna fail.

Wednesday, July 6, 2016

Decided to start me a "window washing" business. Had 500 business cards printed and ordered yesterday and I will get on my grind 1,000% next week when they arrive. I should be able to make it happen from here. As a matter of fact, I know I'm going to make it happen 'cause that's what the fuck I do – make shit happen – accomplish goals, achieve higher levels and make my innervisions manifest into physical realities.

I build shit. I build the visions and images in my mind into real world real life events and circumstances. This is just one more in the long line of visions achieved and many more to come.

Got the wind knocked out of me the other day. A dude I've known for the past 3-4 years, worked with, traded with – told me that he would help "put me back into the trading game" upon my release from The Feds, showed me his true colors. I'm fucked up financially right now and asked if he could send me $500, $1,000, $5,000, $10,000 – anything 'cause I just moved into a new apartment – he told me "no". How could he "really" be willing to put me back in the game with $25,000 - $50,000 to trade and I can't get $100, $500, or $1,000 to get me through the next month?

Once again, people will show their true colors when you need them most. But I'm glad I found out now rather than later. Shit hurt me though. Fucked me up, as I had done so many favors for this dude and when I needed one I couldn't get it. No sweat! – we just keep pushing forward – this shit don't stop! I've been through too much to give up, quit or slow down. The hard part is "ova wit" – losing a $1,200,000 net worth, house, car, businesses then going to the joint for 15.5 months. That shit was difficult!! Starting over is easy and I'm having fun doing it!

I'm a winner! No fuckin' doubt.

Friday, July 8, 2016

Slept good last night. I'm up – updated my charts and read some strong words this morning. Ordered my business cards this week and I will be in motion next week with my squeegee and bucket. I have no fuckin' idea how to wash window but I'm going to start and learn.

I don't know what to expect and I'm scared as a muthaphucka. Scared of failing – scared of not making enough money to live on. I'm looking back at the past. I'm comparing myself to "where I was and used to be", comparing my "insides" to other peoples "outsides".

Instead I should and will focus on my potential with this new life I have. I am 5 months out of the joint. I have a brand new blackboard with a brand new box of chalk. I have total control as to what gets written on that blackboard. It's all new. I have a new life.

Monday, July 11, 2016

Another successful day thus far. Worked out (squats, calfs, quadriceps, dips, Russian twists). Paid some bills, took My Sun to the doctor and ran some other errands. Things are progressing as they should – mostly hard core and sometimes smooth – but progressing nonetheless.

Thursday, July 14, 2016

Started my window washing business yesterday and knocked out 2 clients on the 1st day and signed up another one for a weekly job. Shit is hard work but it ain't harder than FCI Morgantown. It's funny that my first work detail in the joint was "Window Washer" and now – look – I've started a window washing hustle!!

Too funny.

I'm going to give it my all and see what it do. I really just need it to hold me over until I can get my bankruptcy filed and completed. Once that's done then I can start trading options and put my plan down and into effect that I mastered while I was in Morgantown FCI.

I learned so so so much in prison.

Discipline, Patience, mind my own muthaphuckin' business, Concentration, Perseverance, the ability to wait, how to study intensely, physical fitness at the highest level (muscle building and cardio), nutrition and how it affects my body, group dynamics, strength, weakness, courage, fear, boldness, audacity, manhood, loss, gain – the list goes on and on. But most importantly, I was able to renovate and re-define myself, learn myself, know myself – things that I had been unable to do for 45 years prior to leading up to my incarceration.

I made those 15 months, 15 days, 19 hours "serve me" and "work for me" instead of me "serving time." I squeezed every fuckin' drop of water out of the rag. That "life experience" of going to the joint was and is up there with one of the most impactful experiences of my life. I met so so many different people from all walks of life from all over the world (United States Federal Prison) who were "deep down to the core" GOOD PEOPLE – who had just made 1 or 2 bad decisions. I also met some of the smartest and most brilliant people I've ever met in my life. I met some dudes who could this very instant be college professors at the highest level – Ivy League – M.I.T. – you pick one. I mean wizards and geniuses. They are actually – in my opinion – probably more qualified to impart knowledge than any current college professor – as they don't have the distractions of a "free person" in that they can (I did too) study intensely for up to 10 – 13 hours a day, every single day for months and years – I mean really research, examine and get to the very essence of some shit.

I used to love the debates, arguments and dialogue that went on in The Feds. You couldn't just say some shit and you couldn't back it up and prove it. 'Cause another Nigga would go to the library, law library and research that shit to verify what the fuck a Nigga said. These discussions would last for hours and continue for days until all were satisfied that the topic had been dissected to its most minute and granular form.

This part is written on June 24, 2017, as I'm typing this section for publishing and some thoughts came to mind.

I actually miss those types of discussions and debates. They were and are mentally and intellectually stimulating. Out here in society you can't have those types of talks in the course of your day. Everybody is so afraid of everyone else and all fucked up and addicted to their cell phones and the "bullshit information" the internet pumps (tragedy, racism, democrat, republican, war, crime) that most people are "literally afraid" to interact with another human being. Shit is sad.

Saturday, July 16, 2016

Up here in Panera Bread using the FREE WiFi as I don't have internet at home yet. My Sun is playing Starfall on the Ipad and I'm updating my point & figure charts of the /ES, /TF, /NQ, /YM. I lost $1,500 playing poker at the casino Thursday night into Friday morning. I played from 12 noon Thursday until 5am Friday. What was most fucked up is that I was down $1,000, took $500 off my ATM, then got back even and then up $200 and couldn't find it to leave at that point. Then I lost all $1,500 back.

To me – in my own eyes – was most embarrassing and down right foolishness. I allowed this to be a blow to my psyche and self-esteem. I hate the way I felt after that experience as it was reminiscent of the feelings and thoughts of failure I experienced prior to going to The Feds when I had lost all om my material possessions. That at that point meant everything to me (blind as I was to what true & real wealth really is).

I ain't going backwards and that's "hustling backwards". So I'm going to let poker go for now and concentrate on my new window washing business. I got home from the casino at 6am, slept 4 hours and got up and went and did 5 new jobs and made $50 in about 3 hours. That showed me that If I get me my usual 7-8 hours of good solid sleep, proper "fed mentality", energy and a high vibration – I can easily do $100 - $150 in a day washing windows and that what I'm going to do. Put my entire mind on my business and see what I can do wit it! Success no doubt – 'cause that's what the fuck I do!

My Sun has been telling me out the blue lately..."*Daddy I copy you*" and that shit has and is so profound and motivational. In other words, he's watching every move I make. If I quit – he will become a quitter. If I give up – he will learn to give up. If I'm lazy and lethargic – he will copy that too.

But me knowing who the fuck I am and what I'm capable of – he will be fuckin' amazing, strong and will achieve tremendous success – because that's what the fuck I do, have done and will do again. He will actually be 8x better than I am as he has a "real Black American Father" **in** his life to guide, lead, teach, strengthen, mentor and get him ready and right for this Universe.

Monday, July 18, 2016

Came to the Panera Bread to use the FREE Wifi and to write. Lost all the money I had to my name last night in a poker game. Bad move on my part but was a much needed notice to leave that poker shit alone and focus on my new window washing business. I really "don't want to" wash windows – given my reality of just being released from "The Feds" and no employers wanting to fuck with me – it is something I must do.

I went out today and did 5 jobs and verbally got them to commit to "every 2 weeks". Some agreed and some balked – but when I go back in 2 weeks I will close them again. Wasn't big jobs …$5, $5, $5, $10, $6 = $31, but it's mine, its something and it's a start.

I had to borrow $1,000 from my Nigga & frat brutha (Fed Phi Fed) – damn that shit was hard to do – to call that man and tell him I was fucked up and could I borrow a few dollars. Nigga came through for me. Didn't ask no questions other than …Western Union? Money Gram or Bank? This was the same Nigga that sent me my "release clothes" to FCI Morgantown (Nike Suit, draws, socks, t-shirt, dri-fit pullover and sneakers) – a True Friend. You find out who your friends are when you fucked up in the game. You will find out who really loves you and who don't!

Anyway, I'mma make this window washing shit work – put this shit on $100/day by straight flat footed hustlin'. At time I think like - "Damn Nigga you was a millionaire 5 years ago and now you are washing windows – making $5 - $10 a storefront. But the truth & reality is – is that I am now far greater a man than I've ever been. In every facet of the word "Greater". I have more peace of mind, internal strength, focus, drive, energy, discipline and patience. Qualities that I had small tiny amounts of as my financial wealth I allowed to make me soft, reckless, impatient, complacent and feelings of entitlement. None of which are good. Losing it all, going broke and going to The Feds is one of the greatest things that ever happened to me. I was introduced to and found my other "truer self".

Thursday, July 21, 2016

Did Bloomfield Ave, Bloomfield, NJ today with my window cleaning service and did $81...my best day so far! I underpriced one job in particular (Dunkin Donuts) @ $30 when it really was a $90 job. But the owner has 3 locations so my goal was to at least get my chance to show what I can do in order to get all 3 locations. I'm 2 weeks in the window cleaning game – so I have to "give away" some service in order to build the business.

Yo I was doing the shit (window washing) in The Feds for $5.12 a month and even caught a 300 series shot behind this shit. I'm slowly building my route. My goal is to do $100 a day for 5 days a week. That will cover all of my monthly expenses and leave me a little something left over.

Tomorrow will make exactly 6 months of my being released from prison and exactly 6 months left to finish my probation. Sometimes I feel lost and alone. My life "post prison" is so, so, so much different than it was "pre-prison". Or maybe and most likely "it's me" who is so, so, so much different. My thinking – my attitude – my interests – my vision – my goals – my ambition is entirely different. Pussy is not that important anymore as it once was. Trivial bullshit, lack of substance conversations I can no longer tolerate.

When you go to prison – it puts every muthaphuckin' thing into super clear perspective. YOU WILL find out who really loves you and who don't. You will get introduced and discover your other "self". You will find incredible strength – all 3 – (physical, mental and spiritual). You learn that you don't need a bunch of material things or people to be happy. You will discover and find "self-acceptance" in the joint. In "The Feds" every inmate get 300 minutes of telephone talk time per month, $300 of commissary shopping per month, every inmate gets 3 khaki pants, 3 khaki shirts, 5 pair of draws, 5 t-shirts, 3 towels, 1 pillow, 1 set of bed sheets, 1 blanket and your house is a high school locker or smaller with a combination lock. Oh... and 1 pair of black institutional boots.

Now whoever the fuck you was prior to or whatever the fuck you had or where you lived – don't mean a muthaphuckin' thing – you are now a Federal Bureau of Prisons Inmate – and all 1,100 or so dudes on the compound wore and had the same shit! Everybody was equal. So "who you are" is brought to the forefront. So your "word and what the fuck came out of your mouth" had to be backed up by actions. This is when you find out "who you are?".

In The Feds – the inmates are from all over the world. I found this fascinating to watch, observe and conversate with a lot of dudes from different places. I found wizards, highly intelligent geniuses in prison. Dudes that, if given the chance, could come out and day 1 lecture at any school in the United States. I mean muthaphuckas who are brilliant and study things intensely.

I said then and I still say it now, that going to The Feds for the 15 months, 15 days and 19 hours was one of the most impactful and best "life experiences" of my life. TRUE STORY. I fuckin' found myself there! There is nothing I can't do – absolutely nothing. These civilians who sit back and judge an inmate for former inmate cannot – I repeat cannot compete with a prison inmate in the areas of (drive, focus, determination, concentration, mind strength, will, fight, patience, physical fitness, spirituality, mental acuity) – the civilian is outmatched!

It's 9:03pm – "Count time"

On The Pussyness Of The Black American Athlete in 2017

Colin Kaepernick

In my opinion......

Michael Jordan, LeBron James, Kevin Durant, Kyrie Irving, Carmelo Anthony, Kobe, Dr. J, Allen Iverson, Floyd Mayweather, Serena Williams, Venus Williams, Tiger Woods, Draymond Green, Cam Newton, Chris Paul, Charles Barkley, Shaq, Clyde Drexler, George Gervin, Kareem, Akeem Olajuwon, Patrick Ewing, Scottie Pippen, Barry Bonds, Hank Aaron, Jim Brown, Carl Lewis, Sugar Ray Leonard, Marvin Hagler, Tommy Hearns, George Foreman, Deion Sanders, Jerry Rice, Lawrence Taylor, Lynn Swann, Franco Harris, John Stallworth, Drew Pearson, Steph Curry, ………. Too many to continue naming individually... but you get my point.

In other words...

Any living professional Black American Athlete, no matter the sport, regardless of whether you are currently active or retired, male or female... should have called a "joint & unified" press conference and showed up 20, 30, 40, 50, 200 deep with Colin Kaepernick in the middle and showed unwavering solidarity and support for this man for what the fuck he is standing for.

If this had been done.... Colin Kaepernick would have been signed in 24 hours or less. Guaranteed!

Yet these pussy ass, money loving Niggas who need acceptance from others more than "self-acceptance" and "self-love" let this man stand out in the cold by his self. You niggas are weak and ain't shit no matter how much fuckin' money you got..

You muthaphucka's will never be remembered or mentioned with the Muhammad Ali's, Jim Brown's, Kareem's, Bill Russell, Tommie Smith, John Carlos, etc.... This crew is immortal.

Colin Kaepernick did nothing other than say to the entire planet

"I am a Man... I am a Black Man.... I am Somebody"

In my opinion....

Some of the Black Bruthas mentioned ain't no doubt would have been down for sure as they already demonstrated they are back in the 1960's when this was done for Muhammad Ali in Cleveland, Ohio, organized by Jim Brown.

Sunday, July 24, 2016

I am re-living my misfortune of 5 years ago again – now, today, all last week and for the past 3 weeks. Regret, shame, self-beat downs, blame and embarrassment. I thought I had dealt with this in the joint? I thought I had overcome, assassinated and rid myself of this self-manufactured bullshit. I did confront myself and dealt with this shit when I was inside. I did! I made it my business to deal with it. I made it my business to not just deal with the surface thought which precedes the emotion or feeling – I went deep down inside to the cracks and crevices of my soul to uncover and uproot the underlying cause(s). And I did.

However, I think its one thing to be confined in a controlled environment with minimal or no responsibility other than your survival and a whole different thing to be back out in civilization with real responsibilities of providing food, clothing and shelter for me and My Sun to realize and understand how bad I fucked up my financial life. And this is when the regret, shame and self-flagellation emerge. You dumb muthaphucka!

You could've been chillin' hard right now comfortable and laid back. You wouldn't be concerned or worried about paying your rent, cell phone bill, gym fees, etc. But then I examine my current life from another vantage point. As a result of going to The Feds, losing every nickel I had and leaving My Sun – I gained so, so much more that can't be quantified in dollar terms.

I am 47 years old and in the best physical fitness shape of my life. I take no medication for nothing. I learned more about myself than ever before – I mean I really "dug" myself while I was down. All the untrue non-believing, fake muthaphuckas revealed their true selves to me. Conversely, the people who really loved me revealed themselves as well. I learned how much I can take as far as pain, stress, betrayal, loneliness and fatigue. All I lost really was money and material shit. What I gained is immeasurable! I also decided to become an author while I was down. I must have read at least 10,000 – 50,000 pages of books, newspapers, magazines and law material.

I would say I did at least 75,000 – 90,000 push-ups during my entire incarceration (possibly more). I learned about "proper nutrition" and how to really "eat clean" from other inmates who had bodies & physiques that were/are Calvin Klein magazine ready (no gay homo shit).

I learned the importance of going to bed early and rising early and getting at least 7-8 hours sleep. I learned that a 25 – 40 minute nap in the middle of the day is "mental recharge" like no other. There is no better antibiotic, penicillin, medicine, pain reliever, ibuprofen like "proper rest and a good nights sleep". Conversely, lack of rest and lack of sleep can and will fuck your whole entire body and mind around and open you up for fatigue, under performance, stress and sickness.
I learned patience and discipline by watching dudes with 72, 96, 120 , 180, 205, 262, 360 and 393 month sentences get up every day and "walk them days off" and not murmur, complain or whine. That to me was some of the strongest shit I had ever seen in my life.

I learned the art of decision making by playing chess every muthaphuckin' day for hours. Sometimes against dudes who would have high chess ratings by the US Chess Federation if they ever could be rated. And they would all speak of some dude at another prison where they had been who would beat them mercilessly.

I learned how to fight "mentally" and "stay out of the way".

I learned how to trade currency futures while inside. My nigga "Black" was actually trading from inside (British Pound, Japanese Yen, US Dollar, Euro, Canadian Dollar, corn, wheat and soy), he had took a system he ordered from someone he met, tweaked it, "made it his own", and made his own technical analysis charts by hand! He was able to achieve a winning trading percentage of roughly 67% (2 out of every 3 trades were winners). He had to trade conservatively with tight stops and small lots (micros) given his circumstances. I watched this dude and spoke to him everyday for 12 months about trading, money, life, failure, success, will, strength, gangsta shit (him not me), visualization, rebounding upon release from prison, women and so so many more topics. He was serving a 262 month sentence on a drug charge.

I learned so much.

So in actuality, I am in a much better place now than before I got indicted. Yeah I had a $1,200,000 net worth but I was a fuckin' fool, careless, reckless and aimless. Now its different. I am driven, determined, focused, disciplined, patient, careful, tougher and stronger.

All I need now is the $1,200,000 back.

If I did it once I can do it again.

Tuesday, July 26, 2016

My will! That's what its going to come down to. How bad do I really want to make another $1,000,000?

I am willing to do what it takes within the bounds of the law. The pressure is on and the clock is ticking. I want my financial wealth back – I want it back. It feels good to be financially wealthy. That's the last piece. I have My Sun, I am physically, mentally and spiritually wealthy, my vibration is true and my energy is strong. Just don't have the money – but I will in time. I can wait. Nothing wrong with waiting with a plan.

If any nigga can do it – I can! If only 1 person on this planet or in this galaxy can make the comeback – then I'm him – I'm that one! I know I can do it. Let these fearful ass, mediocre loving muthaphuckas talk about what I had and where I am now. Rejoice and laugh cowards. It won't last long 'cause the pendulum is on the "swing back" returning home. The measure of the swing to the right is the exact measure of the swing back to the left. The Principle of Rhythm!

Wednesday, July 27, 2016

Started to write but got too busy getting Lil Sean together

Friday, July 29, 2016

Made $91 yesterday cleaning windows – my best day yet. Still pushing for my first $100 day. I don't like waking up to do windows but once I get out and get started I actually enjoy it. I might be picking up this building as an account – to wash the window 2 per month. I washed one of the tenants who liked my work so much she referred me to the owner of the building.

I've completed 6 months of my 12 months probation. Feels good. My Sun is growing and progressing nicely – he's getting tough. I was roughing him up in wrestling practice the other day. Gittin' that Nigga right!

Ain't no doubt in my mind that I will be a millionaire again. It's going to be sweet! A millionaire 2x in 1 life! I'm determined to make it! You have to believe that shit no matter how bad or adverse things appear or get. Adversity is a good thing. Failure is a good thing and necessary. Embrace it, hug it and make friends with it. Failure is a better more thorough professor than success.

Later that day

Most people are full of fear and afraid to risk even a fraction of what they have to fulfill 100% of their dreams. They discuss other people and events but don't look at themselves and discuss themselves with themself. Pussy ass muthaphuckas!

Even later that same day

If you are a Black American Male and you are the father of a Black American Male child "your life" is over – let me repeat that so you can't say you didn't hear it – "your life" is over. You have made the ultimate sacrifice and now your life is to give your soul to that boy and show him by example the right way. He wants and will copy you. There are no fuckin' excuses – NONE!!

You must do whatever it takes to be a major influence and a material part of his life. No one else on the planet can truly 100% fulfill that duty but you as you provided the cream of life to conceive him. He is you and you are him. His mother, sisters, brothers and relatives must get in the back of the bus when it comes to "him and you" and your responsibility as his Father. You can allow & must compromise at times on some things – but at the end of the day – when it's the 4th quarter with 1 minute left & 2 time outs left or the bottom of the 9th inning with 2 outs and runners in scoring position – "YOU" make the ultimate decisions and that's that.

You wanna know why? 'Cause nobody else on the Planet Earth knows what it is to be a Black American Male in America! Only you can teach, coach, guide and lead him through that! Only you! And that's yo muthaphuckin' job Nigga!

The Black American Nation is counting on you to do that!

In my opinion!

As of this point, for the past 47 years, up to and including this day I haven't and don't take any type of medication for any illness or condition – physical or mental – since I was born. I am in the best physical shape of my life. I workout 7 days a week. My Sun is healthy as well. I and My Sun are together and I see him every day. Money can't touch that! No amount!

I am a wealthy man and I have $34 in my pocket

August 2, 2016

7 – 8 months ago when I was in the joint – my thought and very sincere conviction was that – "I am prepared and willing to work at Mc Donald's and live at the shelter upon my release." If that's where I have to start – then fuck it – that's where I will start. I didn't have to go to the shelter – as I had a lovely and beautiful friend who allowed me to get released to here house and Wendy's wouldn't hire me for $8.75/hour – I guess due to my criminal background, so I didn't even step to Mc Donald's.

I have since started a "window cleaning" business and have my own 2 bedroom apartment. I am doing tremendously better than I was willing to do prior to my release. Faith, effort, energy, will, vibration, focus and determination are real and can make any muthaphuckin' thing possible. I am picking up clients who want me to come "every week", some "every 2 weeks", some "once a month". I had my first $100 day ($111) yesterday. I don't like washing windows but "it's mine and I own my own time". That's what I tell myself while I'm out there and I get frustrated – I say "It's mine!!" and that immediately raises my vibration and pushes me forward.

My Sun is doing good – he is progressing nicely. He can count 7, 8, 9, 10, 11, 12 digit numbers already! I'm on that Nigga hard! I'mma get that Nigga "Right!" I love him. I'm hard on him. Sometimes I wonder if I'm "too hard" on him? Can a Black American Male Father be too hard on his Black American Male Sun? I think not – 'cause America (the good ol USA) – will most definitely be extra hard on him. Slighting him, denying him, ostracizing him, systematically holding him back, mentally trying to weaken his spirit and spiritually attempting to eradicate his will. Nah!!! I can't let him not be prepared for what's headed his way!

I will prepare him!

On another note

The Sun makes up 99% of the mass of the Solar System. It is responsible for light, heat and life itself on Planet Earth.

The Sun is approximately 93,500,000 miles away from Earth.

Nothing is impossible for me!

Thursday, April 4, 2016

"Anything in this world can be done...If you got commitment .... and you got the people to do it and are able to focus upon it" – Rubin *"Hurricane"* Carter

Today I made the "internal decision" to commit myself to my window washing business. Up to this point I have been reluctant to work it to just flat out not wanting and disdaining the idea of me washing windows. I felt it beneath me. I thought thoughts of humiliation to me washing windows.

I would say to myself – "How the fuck did I end up here doing this shit?"
"Damn, Nigga you fell long, far and hard!." – But then I reflect on Niggas I left in The Feds who had 2, 4, 8 more years to go before their release – and I know for a muthaphuckin' fact that – if they were approached with the opportunity to be:

1. Released
2. Reunited with their children (as I have been with My Sun)
3. Have a 2BR apartment
4. Have an automobile
5. Able to go to a real supermarket and buy what they want
6. Able to see civilian women
7. Get some pussy
8. Have a window washing business

Every last one of them Niggas would emphatically reply "Yes!! Absolutely!! Let me have that opportunity and those circumstances!!"

I also saw some Niggas who have been "down" (locked up) 15+ years, 13, 18, 23, 26 years who would also jump at my current circumstance!

So I decided today to stop thinking like a pussy, whining and bitchin' and get the fuck up and make my life whatever the fuck I want it to be. Whatever I want I can bring it into existence! I will spark my 3rd eye illumination and manifest the physical creation!

Saturday, August 6, 2016

Had my best day cleaning windows yesterday ($158). Felt good to know that I can actually make that much in one day. The goal now is to build up my Monday, Tuesday, Wednesday & Thursday to the same level. Then my monthly expenses won't be an issue. Furthermore, the new goal is $200 in one day.

I have to make it! I want my happiness back. It's my responsibility to recapture it. When The Feds came to my office with that search warrant and then the ensuing and consequent events that transpired – it altered forever something inside of me. It grew an anger inside of me that's true and real. The bulk and main crux of the anger is with myself and its constantly aroused when I view my present condition vs. my condition in 2010, on a material level (money, status, cars, real estate).

Why am I here? Why are the material things so important to me? What does that say about me? Am I shallow? Am I justified in feeling the way I feel? Is it normal? I thought I was over this? Am I still looking back – living in the past? How do I eradicate this anger?

By getting back what I lost! That's important to me. Yes it is! I like...no... I love having money. Yes I do. So to get happy again I must "re-earn" my $1,2000,000 that I lost and squandered – mismanaged. I can do it! I'm gonna do it! Shit ain't nuthin' but 315 for 2.... 325 for 2!

Later that same day

I can't give up! If I give up then my suffering is assured to last until I die my physical death. Because if I give up I'm already dead spiritually and mentally – with both being higher forms of existence. When I speak of giving up I don't mean to kill myself or suicide.

No....

What I mean by giving up is "to stop going for mine!" To believe that my dreams are unattainable! To lose my confidence in myself! To be overcome with thoughts of worry and defeat! To settle for where I am in life and just get a job and do what everybody else does!

To allow myself to stop believing that I can do it! To say to myself that "it's too hard!". To let fear win and convince me that I'm incapable. To let my past setbacks, losses and temporary defeats convince me that I'm a failure! To let America tell me that I'm a Nigger, inferior and 2nd class and me buy into and believe that nonsense. To let my felony conviction relegate me to accept employment beneath my qualifications! To live in the past ruminating about shit that has happened, is gone and I can't change! THAT'S GIVNG UP!

I won't give up!

Tuesday, August 9, 2016

Don't have much to say today – just wanted to write something on my book today 'cause I promised myself I would. Went down to Ferry Street (Newark) today and washed some windows. Picked up a few more clients. Gotta keep pushing forward.

Be True!   Be Bold!   Be Aggressive!

Tuesday, August 9, 2016

There is no other place in the 47 years that I've been living, on the 3 continents I've been on, of all the gyms I've worked out at more competitive than the FCI Morgantown "weight pit". I haven't worked out every place on Earth so this is strictly my opinion. Right now I work out at LA Fitness and when I do so I recall & reimagine myself in the weight pit at Morgantown FCI. I haven't been in or seen a more competitive environment.

I never knew what I had in me or what I was capable of until I went to the joint. In the weight pit at Morgantown I got in a "car" with 4-5 other dudes and I worked out with my car every day that wasn't an off day for me. Each day we'd hit a different body part. And when I say we "hit" that body part we would hit that muthaphucka. There was no mercy, pity, acceptance of less than 300%, excuses, injury complaints – no weakness was tolerated whatsoever. I mean Niggas in your car or in another car on the other side of the pit would ride yo ass if you are caught giving less than 4.000%! Niggas will talk shit about your form, the amount of weight you lifting, challenge you that you can't "hit" something (a certain amount of weight) and if you accepted the challenge or bet (which is paid in "macks" or "cans" of mackerel) and miss the weight – man Niggas would fuck with you until you hit that shit.

I thrived in the weight pit! I loved it! I looked forward to it like a high school freshman looks forward to the last day of school.

Bench press or "chest days" was my shit! I had one of the top 10 bench press games in my unit (Gerard Unit – B Wing). My max got as high as 335lbs. I hit 315lbs for 2, 325lbs for 2 and 275lbs for 7 and 225lbs for 17 at the height of my game. I used to talk shit to Niggas and say...

> *"I'm in here for fuckin' up Niggas taxes;*
> *But now*
> *I reppin' Niggas maxes!"*

To rep someones max is to hit it for at least 2 clean reps. I was weighing between 176lbs – 180lbs killing shit in that muthaphucka. In the weight pit you had to "show and prove". Ain't no talkin'! And whatever you said that came out of your mouth about what you could "hit" – you had to back it up in the weight pit. Niggas be serious in the weight pit! We called working out "gittin' money!!".

Tuesday, August 9, 2016

You had to wear steel toe boots in order to work out in the weight pit, either the institutional issued boots, boots off commissary or boots you could buy off a Nigga (contraband) that "hit the hill" and picked up a package. You had to squat, do dips, pull ups, back, everything in your boots.

I worked out in my khaki suit and boots on most week days. Didn't matter whether it was 99 degrees or 11 degrees – a Nigga worked out and got money. The weight pit was outdoors in the open.

I met some Niggas that knew just as much if not more about the anatomy of the human body and nutrition than most doctors of medicine. They knew about muscle damage, muscle repair, training injury. They counted calories, counted carbohydrates, sugar and protein. You knew they knew what they were talking about because they had the body to prove it (no gay no homo shit).

But some of these Niggas had bodies like action figures in a cartoon or toy store. You could see every muthaphuckin' muscle, vein and striation. Niggas were Calvin Klein magazine ready! Word up! Muthaphuckas gave me the game too!! On how to lose weight and lean out. How to cut up or put weight on, bulk up and get stronger. This shit motivated me tremendously to get healthy! When I left Jersey City to fly to FCI Morgantown on October 4, 2014, I was 194lbs, 5' 7", high blood pressure, high cholesterol, high tryglycerides, constant heart burn – acid reflux and gonorrhea. I had 2 chins and Niggas was saying I looked like "a boiled egg with legs". I was fucked up!!

Not to mention the psychological devastation of having to leave My Sun, go to prison, losing a $1,2000,000 net worth ($931,000 in cash), losing my house, tax business, real estate brokers license, real estate business plus the embarrassment and humiliation. I WAS FUCKED UP!!!

When I got to FCI Morgantown and got processed through R&D (receiving and departing (I think that's what it means)) and escorted to my Unit (Gerard Unit – B Wing), I felt a tremendous relief – like a HUGE, gigantic massive weight had been taken off my back. And I began to relax and do my bid.

I started working out from a physical stand point. Immediately did a fearless "internal moral inventory" (written down on paper) – this I did for the entire 15 months 15 days and 19 hours I was in FCI Morgantown. I wrote down what part I played in getting myself where I was. I examined my motives, thought processes, judgement and decisions made – my choices. Why did I do what I did? How did I get here? I stopped blaming things, people and events external to me and took myself to task cutting myself no slack! Prior to going to prison – while I was out on Pre Trial Release – I had become obsessed with "who ratted on me", "who had agreed to testify against me", "who The Feds met with that didn't tell me they did" and "who I thought betrayed me".

Now that shit is real and people did shit to me that I wouldn't have done to them under the same circumstances – but at the end of the day – I put myself in a position to get fucked up and it was all my fault 600%!!! I confronted myself – I checked myself! I chastised myself! I gave myself no mercy – I dug myself! I yoked myself by the collar! And ultimately I had to assassinate "my old self" in order for me to be reborn, renewed and resurrected into a new life form!

I dried my eyes, I picked myself up! I dusted myself off! I patted my ownself on the back! I gave myself a hug! I gave myself some dap! And told myself "You gonna be aight Nigga!" I told myself that I was awesome, amazing, strong, bold, courageous, beautiful and that my best days were in front of me!! I told myself "fuck the past! – no matter of fact – muthaphuck the past!!" It's gone! It's over! Thinking about that shit and holding on to anger, resentment and loss is a complete waste of time and utterly useless!

I told myself that I was a winner! And that if I survived what I went through – that I could do any muthaphuckin' thing I put in my mind! That nothing - I mean nothing was impossible for me! And I meant that shit from the bottom of my soul and the very constitution of my being. And still believe it and always will!

Be True! Be Bold! Be Aggressive!

Wednesday, August 17, 2016

The actual length of the day is 23 hours 56 minutes and 4 seconds

(Stellar day – the actual time it takes Earth to rotate exactly 360 degrees on its axis measured relative to the stars)

The Moon is approximately 250,000 miles from the planet Earth. It's is 33.3% the size of Earth. It rotates west to east. It's radius is approximately 1,086 miles. It is the Earth's only satellite. There is a full Moon every 29 ½ (29.531) days. The moon shines through reflected Sun light. The moon revolves around the Earth from west to east. Rotates about its own axis in about 29 ½ days. Orbits around the Earth in 29 ½ days. "Sidereal Month = 27.322 days" "Synodic Month = 29.531 days (the time between 2 full moons"

The Sun makes up 99% of the mass of the Solar System and lies at the "center" of the Solar System. All the planets and asteroids move around it in elliptical orbits in the same direction as The Sun rotates. Looking down on the system from a vantage point above the North Pole of the Earth, I would see that all the orbital motions are in a "counterclockwise" direction. The Sun is the Mother Star around which Earth revolves once a year (365 ¼) days. **The Sun is the source of light, heat and life itself on Earth.**

The Earth is the 3rd planet outward from The Sun. The mean distance from The Sun is approximately 93,500,000 miles or 149,600,000 kilometers.

Revolution around The Sun	= 365.256 days
Rotation period	= 23.9345 hours
Inclination of equatorial orbit	= 23.45 degrees
Equatorial radius	= 3,986 miles or 6,378.14 km
Polar radius	= 3,986 miles or 6,356.78 km
Number of known satellites	= 1 (the moon)

The Earth orbits The Sun in a path more close to a true circle than most other planets.

The direction of the Earth's revolution – "counterclockwise" – is in the same direction as the rotation of The Sun. The Earth's spin, or rotation about its axis is also in the same direction "counterclockwise"

The tilt (inclination) of the Earth's axis to its orbit (23 ½ degrees), also typical, is responsible for the change of seasons.

Helical fluid motions in the Earth's electrically conducting liquid outer core have an electromagnetic dynamo effect, giving rise to the Earth's magnetic field.

An important characteristic of the Earth's magnetic field is "polarity reversal"
- In this process the direction of the dipole component reverses
  - The North Pole becomes The South Pole

5th largest planet in the Solar System

18.5 miles per hour	= speed Earth orbits The Sun
24,902 miles	= equatorial circumference
197,000,000 sq miles	= total land mass of the Earth
57,000,000 sq miles	= Earth's "land" area (29%)
140,000,000 sq miles	= Earth's "water" area (71%)

1. Knowledge
2. Wisdom
3. Understanding
4. Freedom

5. Justice
6. Equality
7. Food
8. Clothing
9. Shelter
10. Love
11. Peace
12. Happiness

Peace to the Gods!

Friday, August 26, 2016

When you begin to feel that nothing is impossible for you – this is a "corner turn" in your life. I feel this way at this moment. I feel this way because I think this way. Nothing is going to stop me – not even me. I'm done mugging myself, dissin' myself and sabotaging my life.

To believe in yourself is Awesome! Life should be a striving for perpetual self-confidence. You must have an aim! You must have a vision! You must have a destination! You gotta believe! I am a superior being!

I'm on my way back to the top! Not his top..., her top..., their top..., your top...., - My Muthaphuckin' Top! 3 Fold!! It's guaranteed.

I'm that Nigga! I'm the one! If there is only one person in the Universe able to do what I'm about to do – then I am him!

I'mma make a comeback on these Niggas! Watch me!

Sunday, August 28, 2016

I've failed again. I tried to play poker and make my rent money and lost it all "again"! This isn't the right way I should be doing things. I'm sabotaging my own comeback. This is self-inflicted. I'm rushing. I'm in a hurry to get back. I'm not being patient. I'm not giving time...TIME. I have to slow down and take my time. Small steps – in the right direction. One day at a time. Just put together a string of "forward moving one day at a times". I can do it! No doubt about it.

I've done it many times before and I'm even better now than I was then. I'm stronger, healthier, mentally tougher, more disciplined, more aggressive, smarter, wiser – I'm just all around 10x improved.

Take my time and hit my mark.

September 4, 2016

My business is growing big time. I pick up at least 1 new client per week. Picked up 4 last week. My mind is tight. I'm focused and I'm determined to win. Nothing can stop me but me.

Exact Nature

If I tell you exactly who I am, what I am about, the exact nature of myself

Conversely

If you tell me exactly who you are, what you are about, the exact nature of yourself

The Result

We both can save a massive amount of time and get to where we want to go faster.

About 1 month ago I called my "Father" (I guess he is? I'm not 100% sold on it) and told him that now that I am a Father actively participating in My Sun's life that I could and would never treat My Sun the way he treated me. That I can't understand why or how he did some of the things to me that he did. That he treated me fucked up. That wasn't right.

He tried to tell me he loved me – I stopped him instantly and told him "no you didn't" "cause you don't do shit like that to your child". He said that if he had it to do all over again he would do things differently. But reality doesn't let you do it all over again. Once you do it it's done!

He apologized. I said ok. We hung up the phone.

You have to believe in yourself. You have to take risks and fail. Failure is a good thing because it reveals so much. Failure reveals success. Failure shows you "how to". Failure precedes success! (if you don't pussy out and quit)

Monday, September 5, 2016

My Sun starts kindergarten tomorrow. A milestone day for him and me. I will be there. I don't like the fact that he is enrolled at a school with a 4.8% Black population. I'm going to see what it looks like tomorrow and if I don't "feel" what I see then I'm going to make arrangements to have him come to school by me here in Bloomfield, which is way more diverse as far as ethnicity is concerned.

I know his mother is going to resist and fight me tooth and nail on this but I'm ready to war and I'm up to the challenge. She had the momentum prior to my stint in the joint as I was mentally fucked up and legally bound and my whole mind was on not leaving My Sun, not going to prison and saving my life. I was full of anxiety, fear, worry, depression, anger, humiliation, regret, remorse, etc. (all at the same time). You name it I felt it.

But now that's done! I'm renewed. I'm strong. I'm brave. I'm true. I'm bold. I have no legal actions pending (other than a speeding ticket). I'm not fighting for my freedom. I'm a brand new Nigga! Capable of accomplishing any muthaphuckin' thing I want. Whatever I put my mind's eye on - it's done! Ahhhh mna. I'm fuckin' 6x greater than I was before FCI Morgantown – even when I had a $1,200,000 net worth. Yes! "Nothing was impossible for Dantes!". I have cosmic companionship. That is My Sun!! My namesake.

I do not wish to rip him away from his mother and deny her access to him – I only wish to put him in the best possible position to win – and that's with his Father – Me! I am ready for war if necessary.

I picked up another 2 clients today. I have 59 clients in 2 months time. You know I'mma bad muthaphucka! I'm really starting to enjoy window cleaning now. That's a good thing – when you like what you do.

UNITED STATES OF AMERICA   vs   SEAN GUNBY

When that paperwork comes to your mailbox – you open it – and it says "United States of American   vs.   Sean Gunby" – I knew then and there - definitively – that I had fucked up! Lolololol lololololol …. I said to myself that I'm up against a country that deposed dictators, colonized nations/countries, defeated foreign militaries and kills people. DAMN!!!

Fear immediately set in – followed closely by worry, anxiety, panic, insomnia, stress, confusion, bewilderment and fright!! Lololololol ohhh shit! I can laugh about it now but that shit wasn't funny worth a muthaphucka at the time. If you have never experienced this – then you have no idea and cannot even imagine or identify whatsoever.

I have spoken with other men who have "crossed over" and joined the fraternity of "FED-PHI-FED" and all have concurred with this experience of emotions. I did not know then, what I learned 5 years later, that this experience would lay the groundwork for my re-emergence, resurrection, and ultimate comeback and would be my "pivot moment" and one of the greatest experiences of my life.

All of the hurt, anguish and pain along with all of the aforementioned emotions I went through, if I survived it, - and I did – would make me 9x greater that I already was.. and a transmutation would take place propelling me to become and evolve into a superior being - which I am today.

From the day The Feds came with the search warrant to my office (April 14, 2011 – which was 40 days before the birth of My Sun), 17 – 18 deep with those navy blue windbreaker jackets with the yellow letters on the back (IRS-CID, FBI) with bullet proof vests, badges and guns….my thinking and subsequently my life began to spiral downhill quickly. Through my own bad choices, judgement and decision making, my $1,200,000 net worth plummeted down to zero in 15 months. I came close to folding at this point.

Up to this point in my life I equated money with success, status, respect. All of my actions to that point had centered around the acquisition of money and material things. **Money was my religion.** Being born, growing up and living in the United States of America it's hard not to be hypnotized and indoctrinated that money is the primary religion on this continent and thus the majority of the world. So I became a loyal follower and servant of "The Almighty Dollar!". Subjugating and making ride in the backseat was love, respect, brotherly love, compassion and many other noble expressions and qualities in the quest and pursuit of that dollar bill.

I wore $2,200 Hickey Freeman suits, Brooks Brothers suits (from flagship stores on 5th Ave in Manhattan), tailor made suits at $1,200 each, $275 Johnston Murphy shoes (flagship store on 5th Ave, NYC), $90 - $120 dress shirts with monogram, $90 silk ties, smoked $22 cigars at Club Macanudo off Park Ave in NYC, played golf 4x a week, travelled the world, fuckin' around with 7-9 women at the same time, paying their bills to purchase the desire of me and dependence of me – flat out buying their pussy and sexual favors from them. It didn't matter. The money that is – 'cause I made $200,000 in the month of February alone every tax season. So money wasn't a thang!!! I looked up to Goldie and Super Fly as my mentors and tried my best to emulate them. I was lost as a muthaphucka! A fuckin' idiot with money!

Sunday, September 11, 2016

Worked out already today. Didn't sleep all the way through last night. Still don't matter though. I am still going to strive for excellence, accuracy, and precision. This muthaphuckin' shit don't stop! Keep moving forward.

Wednesday, September 14, 2016

Staying focused, determined, brave and strong. Got less than 130 days until I'm off probation. Picking up new clients all the time. Reminding myself to slow my mind down and take my time – in all things. There is no rush. Go slow and get it right.

A real close friend of mine has backed away from me has backed away from me and it's nagging at me. I was and still am very close to this person. I didn't know I would miss her the way I do. Nevertheless, I won't let up on my set up! This shit don't stop. The comeback is in full motion moving forward.

Friday, September 23, 2016

Haven't written in a while. Sean started kindergarten, my window cleaning business has picked up sharply and I continue to exercise and maintain my physical fitness. Yesterday made 9 months being released from The Feds. In 90 days, I'll be off paper for good. It's a wonderful feeling.

Time is very powerful. Time reveals all things. Time is more powerful than Hannibal and his army. Time is real. Time is reality. Time is punctual and precise. Time is accurate. Time is a panacea. Time is truth. I have learned to give time time to do it's job. No need to rush, worry or force solutions.

I am myself's most staunch supporter! I am my #1 fan. I ain't gonna not be with me. I am with me. I got my back. I'm not going to go against me. This is a long way from despising myself – which is a place I once was. I'm back!

Sunday, September 25, 2016

Hustlin' Backwards

This is when you hurt yourself with your own poor judgement, choices, risk taking and decision making. Precisely what I've been doing the last 4 months. In an attempt to pay bills and catch up financially – I've been frequenting the poker room and playing with "desperate money" (money that I can't afford to lose) – I can't "sit right" at the table and play my game the way I know I can and should. Hence, losses mount and I create my own reverse/setback.

I am fully aware of the issue which is the 1st step to overcoming right after acknowledging that there is an issue. My issue stems from my trying to speed up, hasten and fast track my comeback. Bad Muthaphuckin' move!

One day at a time is the proper course of action. Take my time – don't rush! Be patient and wait while I work! Patience!

Thursday, September 29, 2016

I'm writing this book and it feels good. My Sun is doing well in kindergarten. Talking a lot and calling out but doing well. My window cleaning business is growing. I'm going after bigger clients now. No more $3, $5, $8, $10. I want $20 and up. I got less than 4 months left on Federal Probation. Not much to say tonight.

Sunday, October 2, 2016

Here in Newark, NJ at a chess school for My Sun. He is 5 years old. I taught him how to play chess about a month ago and now that's all he wants to do. The other night we played about 13 games straight. I punish him. I pound him. I don't cut the Nigga no slack. I beat him every time we play. The United State of America and the world will do the same to him unless he prepares himself to rise above and prevail. They are not going to "let him win". So why should I?

I don't want him cutting nobody no slack either. Show no mercy. I want him to always know that my dad didn't play around with me, so I'm not going to play around with any of my opponents. I want him to learn and know that "if & when" he does beat me at chess that "if I beat my dad's ass so I'm going to fuckin' destroy you!". I learned to play chess in the 7th or 8th grade, I can't remember exactly. But I really got good when I was in Federal Prison. I would have to believe that some of the best chess players in the world are in prison. I mean we would play chess "all day – every day". I'm talkin' bout competitive – super competitive – shit talkin' – fuckin' over the top – competitive chess! I mean if a Nigga beat you – he would talk shit about your chess game all day, week, month or year until you beat him. Then you gave it back to him. Some niggas were so good that they wouldn't even play you until you beat certain other people. We played for "cans" or "macks" or push-ups. But mostly to talk shit to your opponent if you beat him.

Actually, my 1st bit of self-esteem, confidence and belief in myself started to come back as a result of a chess competition we had in prison. A tournament was organized between Bates Unit and Gerard Unit. Names were drawn and the games were set. I played this dude outta Detroit in the first round. That format was a "race to 5". Whoever won 5 games first won. We played the first day and we split 1-1. A few days later we played again and dude had me down 4-1. I didn't quit, I battled and I fought to even the match at 4-4. The final game we battled and fought. I lost my Queen, - took his Queen later and I ended up checkmating him for the win. I can remember this day as if it was 8 minutes ago. I said checkmate to him and jumped up, the room was ultra-quiet, and said with force "Sean – Gerard Unit – 5-4". Everybody looked up and took notice. The dudes from his unit were surprised as they knew he had me 4-1 and had figured he would win the point. Niggas from my unit were like "Yeahhh Nigga!"

But most importantly, I showed myself that I had it in me to comeback and prevail. To fight and win. That because I was down and losing big – that if I got down, got focused, concentrated and executed – that I could comeback from ANYTHING!! If I could do it in this prison chess tournament – I could absolutely, positively, without a doubt do it in my personal life! This day was a "pivot moment" "turning point" in my psyche and started the healing process.

There was a dude in my unit that had one eye – nevertheless, he was one of the top chess players in the Unit. I called him "Brutha Law". He taught me a lot about chess, chess strategy, tactics, end game and most importantly – chess psychology. He said to me one day "Brutha Sean... *Every move is a kill move.*" *Every move is a kill move!! Every move means something.*" "*What is your opponent trying to do?*" He used to destroy me over and over and over, days, weeks and months. Finally, I beat him, beat him again and my game improved big time. I was never the best in the Unit but I was in the top 7 – 8.

The best player in the Unit always talked shit to me that "Nigga you ain't gonna never beat me before you go home Nigga." I tried, tried and tried and always lost. About a month before I was scheduled to be released (14 months in) I challenged this same nigga to play for some "cans" "macks" (prison currency). He accepted and quickly beat me out of 3 cans. He talked shit to me as well as other players who thought I was out of my fuckin' mind to be playing this nigga for "cans" at chess. That shit only made me more determined. I wasn't going to leave FCI Morgantown without beating this nigga. About 2-3 weeks later I challenged the nigga again to play for some "cans". The very first game – he resigned – before I could checkmate him. I beat him! Another "corner turn" "pivot moment"!

Here not only had I beaten who was considered the best player in the Unit – which was something very few dudes in the Unit could do – but I beat the nigga for "cans". I talked shit to him and made sure everybody in the Unit knew I had beat him. Chess is Awesome!

Friday, October 7, 2016

On this day 2 years ago I woke up in FCI Morgantown, a Federal United States of America Federal Prison for the first time. I was broken mentally, physically and spiritually. I was all the way fucked up! Little did I know at the time that this would be the circumstance and place where God would manifest his infinite oneness and reveal to me that he was orchestrating this entire experience.

FCI Morgantown would be the fertile soil whereby I would plant all new seeds and be reborn, resurrected, renewed and re-emerge as an entirely new, stronger, bolder, deeper and truer human being. I rose as the Phoenix rises. One of the best, if not the best experiences of my life of 47 years.

Today I have tremendous plans and lucid vision emanating from my 3rd eye. Nothing can stop me! Nothing. I will execute my plans and fulfill my dreams. "3 Fold" is guaranteed! 315 for 2! 325 for 2!

I was born March 11, 1969 in Passaic New Jersey at Beth Israel Hospital. My earliest memories are of 77 Lake Ave, Clifton, New Jersey, Apt #8. All 8 families in the building were Black. However, Clifton, New Jersey in the 1970's was very much 96% (or higher) a white town. Racism and prejudice was the modus operandi and the order of the day in Clifton.

I went to Passaic Day Nursery for Pre-K (Jefferson Ave & Columbia Ave, Passaic) and School #12 in the Clifton Public School system for 1st, 2nd and 3rd grades. Me and Timothy Stephens (my best friend) who also lived in my building were the only 2 Black children in the whole school.
But in 1st, 2nd and 3rd grades I had no concept and I think most kids have no concept or recognition of differences, being different, looking different or none of the bullshit that would come later in the 7th grade on up. Kids at that age (1st, 2nd and 3rd) just want to play…play some more… play some more and play again. They don't give a fuck if the other child is light orange with a dark purple ear and fluorescent teeth. They just want to play.

I lived with my mother in a 3-room apartment. My father (I still have my doubts) was there on occasions to beat my mother senseless (black eyes, busted lips and blood all over the floor). I can hear that shit as if it was 9 minutes ago, him telling her, "Bitch, I'll crack your skull" and would commences to beat her with the heel of 1970's platform shoes. I could hear her crying and begging for mercy – but none came – mercy was a no-show. At 5, 6, 7 years old I would pick up the phone and call the police. The 5-O would show up and save my mother from living torture.

At this time, my mother was a "functional work every day" alcoholic. She worked in the health care field. These beating episodes traumatized my mother and me, to an extent I can't even measure. We both lived in terror and fright of this man every night. This fucked me up to the point where my 1st reaction to most anything was fear, shrinking and worry. This plagued me for many, many years and I am certain that it germinated and spawned my drug addiction in the late 80's which almost killed me on several occasions. This living environment, in my opinion, was the impetus for my self-loathing, self-rejection, self-abnegation, low self-esteem, negative self-image and a hundred other mentally debilitating thought processes that haunted me for years and still can if I get off my game.

This dude, my father (if he is?), drove a big long Cadillac with 3 inch white walls, dice in the mirror, 8 track deck with Curtis Mayfield's "SuperFly" flying out of that muthaphucka. He wore big Applejack hats, leather front shirts and sweaters with huge collars, leather pants, long trench coats and had "pork chop side burns" with platform boots and shoes. I guess he would've been considered a "playa" in the 1970's. He smoked "reefa" or "cheeba" (that's what they called it back then), sniffed coke and freebased cocaine. And did all of this in front of me. I had a front row seat. I remember them breaking up manila bags of reefa on album covers separating the stems and seeds and rolling joints and smoking them. I loved to see them hit the joint – hold in the smoke – blow it out making funny noises. I couldn't fuckin' wait to do that. I thought that shit was the coolest shit ever. From those days I bided my time and waited my turn.

October 11, 2016

I've made a decision to remove someone very dear and close to me out of my life. My spirit is in turmoil because I genuinely love this person. This person stood by me in my darkest moments. This individual supported me throughout my prison bit and agreed to let me get released to her home. I really love this person in a unique and special way as a result.

However, things have changed since I've moved out and gotten my own place. The support is no longer there. The friendly vibrations are replaced by contempt. I am not respected any longer as a friend. For this reason or reasons, I have to remove myself. This is new behavior for me. In the past I would try, try, and try, try and try again to fix and solve issues over and over and over again until I became a volunteer for pain. I would accept that kind of mistreatment. But I assassinated that Sean at FCI Morgantown. He doesn't exist anymore. I don't tolerate nothing less than the best for me. There is too too much at stake. Like "JC5" told me "I've been through a lot to be who I am". The stakes are high. My life is at stake. Lil Sean's life is at stake. I ain't got no time to waste.

I'mma get through this probation (102 days left), file bankruptcy and start all over from scratch and win. In time. Take my time and be patient.

But I chose to walk away this time. This is different. Before, the old Sean would think it weak to walk away – but I know now that it is actually a sign of strength, courage, self respect, masculinity, no-nonsense, purpose, resolve and confidence. I am going to miss her but I love me more. I have to. I'mma make it. Wish you the best _ _ _ _ _ _ _! Thank you for everything! I love you! It's ova wit! I've been through too too much to be scared now.

It's my turn. It's my time to win. It ain't my turn to lose no more. It's my turn to win. Fight! Dig! Dig! Figghht! Figghhht! I ain't gonna let up on my set up! I'm not going to go against me! I'm with me! Stand up! I ain't scared no more!

Friday, October 21, 2016

There comes a time and an opportune moment that you can't shrink and run anymore. You can't wait, be patient, exercise restraint, be tolerant, be calculating….. No!

You must STAND, be true, be bold and be aggressive. You have to attack and attack with force. You have to put it all on the line – go all in – even your own existence.

I haven't seen My Sun in 4 days. He hasn't seen me in 4 days. He's looking for me for sure. His mother filed a TRO (Temporary Restraining Order) on me on Tuesday. She recently lost her apartment and is living in the basement of a 1 family, 3 bedroom house with 9 people (5 adults 4 children). My Sun told me that he sleeps in the bed with her sometimes. I checked her that I don't want Sean sleeping in the bed with her. I then asked to let me see his living situation down in the basement. She refused. I called the police to check on the welfare of My Sun. They went and checked. Everything was ok. The next day she filed the TRO.

That's cool with me. Let the games begin. It's time for me to assert myself and let it be known and felt that I am back. I am her and I ain't going nowhere! For too long I had to let things slide and couldn't make any real moves in "My Sun's" life as I was tied up with my Fed case and his mother knew that and pimped that to the fullest. But now things have changed. I'm on a "91 day countdown" to being off federal probation and totally done with that entire Fed case! I'm here and I'm going to be here.

It's my turn to win – it ain't my turn to lose no more. Yeap! I will get full custody of My Sun. I ain't takin' no shorts, having no pity or mercy. She didn't have none on me. I feel confident and strong. I've prepared for this event for a long long time. I'm ready!

Sunday, October 23, 2016

It's an amazing feeling when you actually see and feel your own "growth & progress" right before your eyes in action and in real time. When things that used to fuck with me and knock me all the way off my square and out of my tree – no longer do 'cause I've done the necessary internal work on myself.... I've done a fuckin' deep searching, fearless, extensive, deep spiritual & mental inventory, assessment and self-examination. Cutting myself no slack and showing myself no mercy and no pity at all. I did it. I did it with the intent of helping myself, improving myself, improving my performance, elevating my game and rising to new heights. It worked! I'm infinitely stronger, better, more patient, wiser, more robust, deeper and more disciplined than I've ever been. I can't be stopped! I got to be the baddest muthaphucka that ever visited the Planet Earth!

Thursday, October 27, 2016

I'm on an "85 day countdown" to being off Federal Supervised Release (Probation) and it feels good. I will make it. It's been 5 years 7 months since it all began and one the Greatest Experiences of my life.

Sean's mother filed a Temporary Restraining Order against me last Tuesday. I haven't seen my son in 10 days. This is the longest we've been apart since my release from prison. I know he has been looking for me. It's ok. I didn't respond or "react" in a way that would get me fucked up even more. I didn't call her, go to Sean's school or nothing.

I went to pick him up last Tuesday and was told that he was picked up already and that a restraining order had been filed against me and that I could not pick him up any longer. Man.... I was cool as a fan – got in my truck and came home. I'm sure his mother expected me to "go off", get emotional and call her phone, go to where she is living (homeless again for the 3rd time in 8 years) and get wild.

WRONG!!!

Not today!

3 – 4 years ago that is precisely how I would have responded…. Got arrested, went to jail, made a "civil" Temporary Restraining Order into a "criminal" Permanent Restraining Order and really give her ultimate control of My Sun….

Naahhhh bitch you can't get that!! I know I just didn't do 16 months in Federal Prison to come out and let you fuck me up again. Naahhhh! I learned too much in The Feds about "waiting", "patience", "discipline" and being a crash dummy watching other niggas do dumb brainless shit to get themselves locked in "the jail inside a jail" (the SHU). Plus I know you cooperated with The Feds against me and you own child. You dumb weak muthaphucka! I know you did. But hey – what goes around comes around and karma is a bitch. What you do to people comes back to you. What you throw out into The Universe will come back to you with mathematical exactness!

I have an attorney and the hearing is next week for the TRO. It will get lifted and I'll pick Lil Sean up and get back to my business of being a Black American Male Father to a Black American Male Sun….. The best, most important and toughest jobs on the Planet Earth.

November 14, 2016

Went to court today for the TRO and Sean's mother requested an adjournment to get help from legal aid. New court date is December 14, 2016 (30 days away). Didn't expect this. Caught me off guard. My attorney as well.

My expectation was to pick up Sean tomorrow. It's ok. I'm disappointed but not discouraged. I'm strong and firm and steady. 30 days ain't shit!! And I'm free – shit. I waited 477 days to see him while I was in the joint – so "30 days on the street" ain't shit. I cultivated my ability to wait in prison. Not an issue. The TRO is full of fabrications and lies. But hay – this is what she likes.

I miss My Sun. I know he misses me. In time…. Soon.

On another note, a woman that I have been involved with for 5+ years has been verbally abusive toward me since I moved out of her house and got my own place. Tonight, she called me a "bitch".... WHOA!! Those are fighting words. This was over the phone. I had been staying loyal to her as she did my whole bid with me and let me get released to her house. I feel or felt that "I owed her" never ending loyalty for that and have been putting up with her verbal abuse based on that principle. But tonight it has gone too too far. The respect is not there. She does not respect me. I know that when a woman begins to talk to her man like that - that "it's over". No need for me to slap the shit out of her or put my hands on her. Just removed myself – that's all. It's easy. I'm 67 days short from being off paper with The Feds.... Ain't no room for this type of energy.

Anyway, I'm strong – tight mentally – focused, determined and will win. It's good to be me!

Saturday, November 19, 2016

I haven't seen My Sun in 32 days. This is the longest we've been apart since my release from prison. I am lonely. I am hurting. My vibration is down. I miss him. That's "My Main Man!"

However, I still remain strong, energetic and positive. I continue to put "good clean" foods into my body and get my 7 – 8 sleep per night. These 2 put together on a consistent basis is better than any health coverage plan that can be purchased.

I did my biggest job "window cleaning" today ever. $150 for one job. Took me 3.5 hours to do. My business is growing every day.

I remain motivated, focused and determined. I'm on a "62 day countdown" to getting off Federal Supervised Release.

Spoke to my man Victor today on "What to do to win"

1. Don't smoke
2. Don't drink
3. Moderate TV & music consumption
4. Moderate sexual activity
5. More input into the PC (computer) vs. what you take in or output from the PC
6. Proper sleep
7. Exercise and diet
8. Be keenly aware of your social circle

9. Program yourself @ night with meditation and deep reflective thought to awaken the next day more confident and better programming

Wednesday, December 7, 2016

It has been exactly 51 days since I've seen My Sun, Lil Sean, Sean X. Gunby, Jr. I miss him deeply and it has begun to affect me physically. The stress. I miss his vibration – his energy. I know for a fact he misses me too. His mother put a frivolous Temporary Restraining Order against me full of lies, omissions and slander. There was no physical altercation. Just her "attempting" (unsuccessfully) to get me off my square and separate me from my child. Her guilt, fears and insecurity is and has been the driving force behind her deliberate pernicious attempts to bury me, to hurt me, destroy me, ruin me and ultimately kill me.

Oh but she has miscalculated. She is under the impression that I am the Sean Xavier Gunby of 3 – 4 years ago. The Sean X. Gunby, Sr. that would get super emotional and react irrationally. The impulsive, reckless Sean X. Gunby with no trace of restraint, self-discipline, patience or wisdom. But you see, I killed him. He no longer exists. He's done away with. Today, I am the renovated, rebuilt, redefined, reborn and resurrected Sean X. Gunby, Sr. The likes she has never seen.

However, she will get to experience first hand this new "Over Man". She has no idea what is about to transpire, what is coming her way. I will lead a charge, crusade, campaign and war against her she never thought possible. It will be rapacious, speedy, deliberate, calculated, aggressive, everlasting and relentless. I want revenge and I'm going to get it. She will regret the day that she was born when I'm done. I am going to break her. I will win! Guaranteed. And I'm ready to die for My Sun, Sean Jr.

Peace Out!

Be True!
Be Bold!
Be Aggressive!

December 25, 2016, Sunday

Today is the 1st Christmas I've spent with My Sun in 3 years. I missed the last 2 due to my incarceration. I bought him or "Santa" brought him a Spiderman bike. Well, "Mee Ma" (Grandmother) actually bought it for him. These moments are so special and in my opinion are the best things in life.

I'm currently in a custody battle for My Sun and I'm going to prevail. I'm going hard and cuttin' nobody no slack! Muthaphucka's didn't cut me none. I'm ready and I've prepared for this. I realize now (by looking backwards) that everything I've been through in the last 5 years 8 months has been training and preparation for this moment. Without losing all the possessions that I owned and going to Federal Prison (a place where I remade, renovated and rebuilt myself), I wouldn't have had the mental, spiritual and physical endurance & stamina to undertake this task. I now see that it was all necessary. This is a scary situation and takes a tremendous amount of courage. But so did walking a Federal Prison yard after you've had words with another inmate. I did that so I know I can do this!

Be True!
Be Bold!
Be Aggressive!

Sunday, April 16, 2017

This shit don't stop. It's always a "mind set", and that mind set is in the control of the individual. You will have a "losing or weak mind set" and your life will reflect same or you will have a "dominant winning mind set" and your life will reflect this. It's up to me. I have a plan. I know where I am going. I have a map. I have an itinerary. I am on this muthaphucka hard core too. Nothing is going to distract me from where I want to go. Nothing! No money, no relationship, pussy, electronic device, poor health, person, place or thing. No situation, no circumstance, family member, nothing or nobody will stop this muthaphuckin' Master Plan that I got.

I believe in me 6,000%!

Thursday, April 20, 2017

You have to continually "turn your game up" to meet challenges and rise to the attainment of any of your goals. This is done every day, within a day, within the hour, within the minute or seconds. This shit don't ever stop. When it stops... when you stop elevating your game ...you fucked up. Something killed you, someone destroyed you, some event, some circumstance, some person, some place or thing has killed you. You are still walking around living, breathing, working but you are just existing. You have been dead a long time ago.

It's only the "real niggas" that perform alchemy and are true alchemists. They take whatever the fuck happens, whatever the fuck comes, whatever circumstance, whatever weak ass hatin' ass niggas that come at them and they raise their vibration, elevate their frequency, strengthen their spirit and resolve........they elevate, they rise and they transmute and transform that which is undesirable into that which is valuable and they win!

This shit don't stop!

Sunday, April 23, 2017

We must and will continue to push forward. With self-talk and "speaking it up" what it is we will do and what we will accomplish makes it only a matter of time. I speak up where I will be. I speak it to myself in the affirmative. I am very definitive in my self-talk... very direct... very matter of fact. This is real. This is no Sesame Street.

I am better than the over whelming majority of the people that I see in society. I will not shy away from speaking same just because it's not "being humble" to say such a thing. Or the other one... "you are arrogant!". So what. Fuck what you think. I don't live for you.. I live my own life. I reject that mental poison that this country and school system taught me that "all men are created equal". Bullshit. (save the people born handicapped, mental illness, retardation, etc.). But for everyone else. Bullshit. Some people ain't shit. Some people are better than other people. I for one am one of them.

I love being me. It's good to be me!

Tuesday, May 2, 2017

Success is not lured. Success will not come to you if you ask it to. Success will not come if you invite it. Success will not answer the phone, email or text. That Muthaphucka must be captured. Success has to be tackled and put in a choke hold. You gotta go get that Muthaphucka.

Saturday, May 06, 2017

Got a very important goal accomplished this past week. I filed my bankruptcy. Upon my discharge from bankruptcy, I'm freed up to really get involved in the entrepreneurial pursuits I love, most notably, real estate investing and options trading. It will be time to put down and execute my "Master Plan" that I mapped out and worked on in The Feds. Now it's just a waiting game. I know how to do that.

Still cleaning windows and that shit is constantly growing and I've started to enjoy doing it.

Still working out 5-7 days a week, eating clean, working on my goals and resting. My continued success is guaranteed.

Wednesday, May 10, 2017

A Nigga look good, is thinking good, feeling good and living good. This muthaphuckin' shit don't stop! Every day I move forward and toward my objective. Nothing is impossible for Sean G! A nigga cleaning these windows, working out, eating clean, getting 7-8 hours of sleep per night, thinking positive powerful strong thoughts. Envisioning my life as I want it to be and setting about the task of accomplishing each goal ONE AT A MUTHAPHUCKIN' TIME, thereby, manifesting my thoughts into physical material reality for the world to see.

I love the muthaphuckas who hate me and have sworn to themselves that they will destroy me. These faggot ass weak ass niggas keep me sharp, focused, disciplined and patient. 'Cause ain't no muthaphuckin' way I'mma let these sucka-ass niggas "out success" me or beat me.

I stand my ground and get down for my crown. That's it. I'm going to die one day so fuck it and fuck what anybody thinks, feels or says. Fuck 'em. This is my muthaphuckin' life. **I have a right to my life!**

I'm 18x stronger than I've ever been. I am fuckin' unstoppable!! All I have to do is think it and it manifests in reality.

I will get back. Guaranteed!

Thursday, June 01, 2017

It is muy importante that I stay in control of how I perceive me. I have to mentally control "my own perception of myself" or else be subjected to how someone else or others perceive me - this is a horrible mental condition.
Being physically fit is of utmost importance. If you feel good then you look good. If you think good then you feel good. Physical health is more valuable than any amount of money imaginable. I must control what I think and what I eat. A regularly scheduled exercise program is of supreme importance.

Turn the TV off. Turn the phone off. Turn the computer off. Doing this quiets the mind and allows for deep penetrating thought, contemplation and decision making. It also affords time for completing house work, paperwork, paying bills, reading, meditation, napping, resting, sleeping and flat out peace of mind. This is outstanding for mental health.

On Morris Brown College in the late 1980's:

I had graduated from Clifton High School in Clifton, New Jersey that summer of 1987. My mother had been saying for years prior *"you going to Morris Brown... my brother Sunt went to Morris Brown... you going to Morris Brown"*. I'm like any teenager at the time thinking *"ok... whatever you say.. can I go outside and play?"*

Well in August 1987, I checked into Borders Towers, Room 306, a dormitory on the campus of Morris Brown College in Atlanta, Georgia. My mother was right.. I was not only going to Morris Brown .. I was at and enrolled as a freshman at Morris Brown College.

Let me expound and elucidate on the history and background on Morris Brown College. Morris Brown College is a Historically Black College and University and at the time was a member of the Atlanta University Center comprising the schools of Morris Brown, Morehouse College, Clark College, Interdenominational Seminary (ITC), Spelman College and Atlanta University. All classes and credits were transferable between the different institutions so that a Spelman student could take an Accounting class at Clark College and a Morehouse student could take a Business Law class at Morris Brown and the credits would be transferable. Together these schools comprised the largest institution for higher education for Black people in the entire world.

Morris Brown College was founded in 1881 (16 – 18 years after the signing and implementation of the Emancipation Proclamation) by a man named Morris Brown who organized an A.M.E. church in Charleston, South Carolina. However, in 1822, a slave revolt led by Denmark Vesey and Jack Gullack brought a lot of pressure on the congregation of free blacks anywhere in Charleston, SC.

As a result , Morris Brown migrated up north to Philadelphia, Pennsylvania where he opened a boot-and-shoe making business.

He eventually returned to Atlanta and founded Morris Brown College. Morris Brown College is the **ONLY** institution for higher education in the State of Georgia founded by Blacks for Blacks! No other school in Georgia can lay stake to that claim. On Mo Brown!!!

The first Black Principal in the Atlanta Public School (Washington High) system was a Morris Brown graduate.

The first Black teacher in the Atlanta Public School system was a Morris Brown graduate.

The first Black secretary in the Atlanta Public School system was a Morris Brown graduate.

The oldest Black owned and operated business in Atlanta was founded by a Morris Brown graduate. (Frazier's Café Society)

Alberta Williams King, 1938, is a Morris Brown graduate. This is Martin Luther King, Jr's mother.

A lot of Martin Luther King, Jr's lieutenants and close confidants were Morris Brown graduates.

The first football player to get drafted by an NFL team from the AUC schools came out of Morris Brown. (Ezra Johnson) Green Bay Packers

"Morris Brown College is deeply rooted in the soil of self-help and for a period of nearly one hundred years has continued steadfastly its work of establishing race pride, building men and women for service, notwithstanding several periods of crises."

Morris Brown College, The First Hundred Years, by Sewell and Troup, PREFACE

"Morris Brown College grew out of the efforts of Negro people to help themselves, and even though the growth of the institution has been such that outside help became advisedly acceptable in later years, it only emphasizes the value of the self-help that brought the school into being."

Morris Brown College, The First Hundred Years, by Sewell and Troup, page 6

"But perhaps the most significant contribution that Morris Brown College has made to the past history of Negro education, perhaps the most significant contribution this college can ever make to the development of the Negro in America is to fight for existence as a check and balance against forces in American life which would still in this year of 1934 and even later, seek to compromise on the intellectual, social and economic stature of Negro people. No thinking people can doubt that there is a group, supposedly friendly to the American Negro, which expects to surrender to the Negro only a limited place in the sun. Such a group makes the thinker question his friendship and simultaneously develop uncompromising loyalty for institutions like Morris Brown College, institutions which cannot see compromise in truth."

There are many other contributions that Morris Brown alumni have made to Atlanta, GA and the world.

Getting back to my story…..

After I checked into Borders Towers and found my dorm room and got situated, my mother and I went to the West End section of Atlanta and opened me up a checking account. She put $400 in it, I got me a Tillie Card (ATM card) and that was that. She stayed 1 more day and then said "I'll see you later"……

There I was 18 years old, 856 miles away from Clifton, NJ, didn't know how to wash clothes, a stranger to the city of Atlanta on a college campus, on my own. At this stage of the game I was a straight up "mama's boy" and didn't know how to do shit for myself. That's why I am thankful to this day that my mother did what she did… took me to Atlanta, dropped me off with $400 and said "I'll see you later!"…. I had to learn how to take care of me. This was one of those "pivot moments" in my life. I got a job caddying at Atlanta Country Club and other part-time jobs and set about the task of taking care of me. I have never went back home to live with my mother since except for a few months after I dropped out of college due to my drug addiction. Other than that I've been out in this world on my own since 18 years old and never looked back.

Morris Brown College in the late 1980's was the spot to be. Atlanta, GA in the late 1980's was the spot to be for young Black people. There were young Black people there from all over the United States and the world. At this time, Atlanta, in my opinion, had the finest, most beautiful Black women on the planet Earth. I was not the only Brutha who had this opinion, most Brutha's there uttered the same sentiments. Man these women were bad. Physically gorgeous and were in college to boot. Even the native Georgia Peaches were dope!

During this time, Hip Hop Music was pro-Black in it's message and it was all about knowledge of self and being proud to be Black. Hip Hop music in the late 1980's was a history class/lesson, a civil rights march, religion, a Black Panther rally, Africa, Malcolm X, Dr. King, H. Rap Brown, Angela Davis, etc, etc., etc., all rolled up into one massive oratory with leading rappers like Chuck D, Flava Flav, KRS-ONE, Big Daddy Kane, X-Clan, Eric B. & Rakim, N.W.A., Eazy E, Ice Cube. But in my opinion, the most revolutionary Hip Hop group ever was Public Enemy without question. Chuck D's cadence would put me into a hypnotic trance and make me stop what I was doing and rewind the cassette 14x to really make sure I heard what he said. Then I would go to the dictionary and library to research what the fuck I just heard. This Hip Hop era sparked some serious conversations and dialogue on Black College campuses for sure but I know for a fact it did at MoBrown!!! Niggas would sit on the wall or in front of the towers or on the yard and talk about "what's really going on!!" and it all came from Hip Hop!

Big Daddy Kane was another Nigga that had me at attention. In my opinion, one of the dopest MC's ever!!!! Nobody flowed like KANE (King Asiatic Nobody's Equal)... fast rhyming, slow rhyming, stringing along words, syllables, metaphors... Nigga was nice wit it!!

Boogie Down Productions/KRSONE was on some other shit. This Nigga really had me in the Woodruff library cracking open encyclopedia's and history books and shit. "The TEACHA!!!"... My Philosophy, Why Is That?, You Must Learn, ahhhhhh man... When this Nigga spoke you sat up like a Doberman pinscher in the front seat!! He really had something to say.

X-Clan... "This is protected by the RED, the BLACK and the GREEN....with a KEY ... SISSSSSSYYYYYYYY!.... Ah man... these dudes were for real about that Black Shit! Brutha J was a lyrical master not only speaking on Black American history but Ancient Egyptian-Nubian African history. The Sun, Moon and Stars... The Cosmos... Ahhhhh man... Then Professor X would bogart his way into the vibration with his authentic voice and call on Malcolm X, Marcus Garvey, Huey Newton and H. Rap Brown to meet him at the crossroads!!!!....... Wow!!!

Rakim is a Bad Muthaphucka!!! My senior year in high school in 1986 – 1987 dropped Paid in Full the album. "I Ain't No Joke" would get played in my ride back-to-back-to-back-to-back-to-back. You can put that song up against ANY MUTHAPHUCKIN HIP HOP RECORD EVER MADE and it will hold it's own... In my opinion.... Niggaz don't give Eric B the credit he deserves though cause that production and them beats were PERFECT for Rakim. FOLLOW THE LEADER!!

I fucks with MC Shan too... Fuck dat.. MC SHAN was a dope muthaphucka period. And In my opinion, didn't lose the battle to KRS-ONE but held his own and told them Nigga to "KILL THAT NOISE".... The track "Down By Law" is one of my all time favorite Hip Hop records... My Sun (6 years old) loves MC SHAN... "MC SPACE"... "LIVIN IN THE WORLD OF HIP HOP".... A true Hip Hop pioneer...

Then these Nigga from the West Coast came on the set in 1987 -1988 talking some totally different, no holds barred, straight to yo face, "Straight Outta Compton" shit. Now during this time, there was no West Coast, Dirty South, Mid West rap... NYC and Jersey dominated the Hip Hop world... so I was like "who are these niggas?"... Well Ice Cube, Ren and Eazy let muthaphuckas know exactly who they were. This was a "pivot moment" in Hip Hop. Eazy E was the first you Black male I saw that had his own label (Ruthless Records) and was the Executive Producer of an album. He was serious!

At this time in Hip Hop to get on the mic, radio and MTV Raps **_"you had to have something to say"_**... At this time Hip Hop music was controlled by the very people that invented it ...The Young Black American Male"... Mr. Magic, Red Alert, Chuck Chillout, Marley Marl, Russell Simmons and Rick Rubin (white boy... and a Bad Muthaphucka)... You couldn't just get shot, have a prison record and mumble shit on the mic... You also had to have ORIGINALITY!!! You had to have your own style and not copy another muthaphucka!!!

This era of Hip Hop from (1983 – 1988) was THE MUTHAPHUCKIN TRUTH! There were some lyrical monsters out there and a lot of these MC's today wouldn't have made it. Jay Z couldn't make it then... He used to open up for Big Daddy Kane and is in the same age group as those very MC's from this era and he was a nobody then.

Also at this time in NYC, Hip Hop was only played on the radio 2 nights a week for 3 hours ... (Friday & Saturday nights from 9pm – 12 midnight)... That was all the Hip Hop you got all week except for groups like Whodini and Run DMC would get some radio play. But for the most part it was Friday and Saturday nights...

I remember going to music stores (Record City in Passaic) or Coconuts and getting me a fresh Maxell or Memorex "Gold Coaxial Chrome" cassette and sitting by my box at 8:45pm getting my tape ready to record as soon at Red Alert played that siren or Mr. Magic played Whodini's Mr. Magic Rap Attack... 98.7 KISS or 107.5 WBLS... There was also a radio station in NYC called 92 KTU that was nice. I would sit there and "make me a tape" to listen too for the whole week until next Friday. That was the shit... All my tapes were DOPE!! I still have some of them shits....

If you didn't live in the NYC Metropolitan area during this era you missed it ... Straight up... There's no other way to put it... The subway trains were all graffiti'd out from top to bottom, inside the car, on the windows, on the ceiling everywhere... Graffiti was everywhere on every pulled down bodega gate, every wall, EVERYWHERE... Times Square – 42nd Street was no joke. When you came out of Port Authority in the 1980's .. to walk from 8th Avenue to 7th Avenue on "40 Duece" was an experience. Peep shows, prostitutes, drug addicts, hustlers, crack addicts forcibly washing peoples car windshields at the red light. New York was NEW YORK back then. When you went up to Harlem, you could buy weed without getting out of your car. Niggaz (3 -4 niggaz) would run up to your car and serve you fat nickels of weed. My spot was 145th and Edgecomb. I used to buy 20 nickels for $100.. the dreadlock man would "kick" me another 3 on the strength and I would bring them back to Jersey and sell them for $10 and double my money and have weed to smoke... lolololol....

Then crack hit and shit really went left. I think in 1988 and 1989 there were over 1,800 – 1,900 homicides per year in NYC. You would turn on the news at 6pm and there would be 3 – 7 murders per day/night in NYC. Shit was crazy. Thank god I made it through that shit...

RUBIN "HURRICANE" CARTER

"Anything in this world can be done …. if you got commitment and you got the people to do it and are able to focus upon it"

On the Black American Male Athlete:

History reflects and has recorded that this certain, particular homo sapien sapien, located on the continent of what is today called North America, the United States of America or America is the most dominant and supreme athlete on the planet Earth.

Me being a member of this group, I have made a serious attempt to be as impartial, non-biased and as neutral as I possibly can when I've analyzed this thought (or fact) so as to keep it real and really determine and conclude if this is so.

I am 48 years as of the writing of this document and what I have witnessed with my own eyes this has to be the case. The Black American Male athlete is the baddest Muthaphucka on the planet Earth when it comes down to competing with physicality, strength and will in a sporting event. It goes without saying. Is it even up for discussion? I mean when a "Brutha from America", "a Nigga" or "Black Man from America" (whatever you want to call him) makes up his mind that he is going to excel at this particular sport or that particular sport and takes the court, field, baseball diamond, track or whatever the venue no other homo sapien sapien from any other ethnic group nowhere in the world can fuck with him! NOBODY! Europe, South America, Africa, Asia, America, Caribbean. NOBODY...NOBODY...NOBODY can do what he does. A Nigga will take it to a whole nother level, plane or dimension.

Let's examine this together...

Muhammad Ali, Hank Aaron, Jim Brown, Kobe Bryant, Willie Mays, Satchel Paige, Lawrence Taylor, Reggie Jackson, Kareem Abdul Jabbar, Michael Jordan, Jesse Owens, Barry Bonds, Bob Gibson, Lou Brock, Bo Jackson

At first the Black American Male Athlete wasn't allowed to play football, baseball, track and field or basketball. Once allowed to participate the shit was over. If hockey and golf didn't require a serious financial commitment to play then those would be dominated by the Black American Male Athlete also. Tennis the same thing.

I remember growing up in Jersey in the 1970's and 1980's watching the New York Yankees start 4 -5 Black players every night, every game (Chambliss, Randolph, Rivers, Jackson, White, Gamble). In fact, during this era the National League would win more as they had more Black American players than the American League. And back then, the players "PLAYED" the All-Star game it wasn't some exhibition like it is now where all the players get together laugh and smile and "take it easy" on each other...

In my opinion, today's baseball in 2017 is not the "highest" level of baseball because the Black American Male Athlete is missing. Black Dominicans, Black Cubans, Black Venezuelans or Black Africans are "Black" but they can't fuck with a "Black Nigga Athlete" from America! NO WAY NO HOW!!! It's something about the "Black Nigga Athlete" from America. He is different than all other Blacks on the planet. He's more dominant, stronger, faster, more aggressive, physically superior, tougher, meaner, quicker... He's on whole nother level, plane or dimension.

You have white pitchers, Dominican, Cuban or wherever pitchers throwing the ball 98 – 99mph. Ain't no doubt in my mind that some "Nigga" somewhere in America (prison, drug game, drug user or maybe just working) that if developed and guided properly could throw a baseball 108 – 112 mph easy. The art of stealing bases in baseball is a dead art because the "Nigga" ain't in the game. Back in the 1970's – 1980's, man base stealing was the shit. This added a whole nother concept to 9 innings of baseball. The pitcher had to be forever vigilant of the "Nigga" on 1st base because he knew, the catcher knew, the umpire new, both head coaches knew, every player on the bench knew and every fan new that that "Nigga" was going to steal second base and there was nothing that anybody could do about it. He was just too fuckin' fast. Then he was going to 3rd!! and may even steal home if you fuck up.

To me, that was baseball. The speed element was forever present.

Babe Ruth, Ty Cobb, Mickey Mantle or any of those hyped up white players did not play against Black ball players so this means that they did not play against the best. Hence, their records, stats and achievements have asterisks next to them.

2 Black American Males broke Babe Ruth's home run record. Hank Aaron did it under the threat of death to himself and his children as he got closer to the record. Barry Bonds did it under the "media character assassination".

Swimming ... forget about it... Soccer... any sport.. ANY SPORT... give a "Black American Male Athlete" or a "Nigga" equal access to it and he takes it over instantly and it can't be stopped. That's just the way that it is and that is real.

Anyway, that's how the fuck I feel about it...

On Dr. King's Thesis of Integration:

When one honestly examines the current state of affairs and condition of Black America (economic, physical health, mental health, unity, aim, direction, purpose, agenda, plan, road map, itinerary) and it's members, one must conclude that Dr. Martin Luther King Jr's. thesis and belief in the integration of the Black American into main stream white America has been a colossal failure, In my opinion.

Let's examine this....

Look at where we are as a "collective group". We are nowhere. We are here in America constantly being treated with disdain and contempt. There is no "Black American Leadership". We have no compass, no map and are utterly aimless. Our leadership is the "white American elite". How ridiculous is that? We have no agenda. How could it ever be that the white American elite's agenda and future plans ever align with Black America? It will never be. It is impossible as we are 2 entirely different people.

Today in America Black people are over-weight, fat and obese and for all intents and purposes unhealthy. Mental illness is rampant in Black America. Incarceration in "private prisons" of young Black males is astronomical relative to our comparative population in the USA. Unemployment. The educational system here in America has and will continue to fail Black America.

White police officers have waged all out war against Black men. A white police officer can shoot and kill an unarmed Black man without any type of repercussion or consequences.

I mean look at where we are. What are we doing? Where are we going?

In my opinion, Dr. King was a good solid dude. Dr. King was a real Nigga who loved Nigga's. He really loved Black people and willingly gave his human existence "life" up for Black people. My mother taught me about Dr. King way back in the 70's and I've been a follower and admirer of Dr. King since. I would always take his birthday off from school back in the 1970's – 1980's before it became a national holiday. I "fucks wit" Dr. King. I love Dr. King as he loved me before I was even born. However, at the end of the day, he thesis and push for Black American integration into white America was a failure. In my opinion.

On Malcolm X's Thesis of Black Separation:

We never will know whether this would have been a success or failure? Malcolm was against integration and pushed for "the Black man must help himself". The Black American must separate from the white man and "solve his own problems his-self". This makes sense to me.

Let's examine this...

In a marriage, 2 people live together and share their lives with each other. In some marriages, (not all but most) there comes a time when these 2 people just can live together anymore, they have fallen out of love, they are no longer having sex, they are sleeping in different rooms, both are having affairs, they walk through the house and don't speak to each other, verbal fights, physical fights etc.. The situation if just fucked up and neither party is happy and there comes a point to where the "solution" for both parties is to separate and go their separate ways. Quizzically, most times, after the separation these 2 people become the best of friends, confidants, supporters and learn to respect each other again.

Currently, white America and Black America are in a marriage that is long past it's expiration. White America (not all) for the most part doesn't want us here. This is shown by the segregation, police brutality and mass incarceration rates of Black men. Black people shouldn't want to be where they are shown no respect and mistreated. This is the white man's land. He holds the power. (I know some Niggas gonna say "we built the is muthaphucka man.. We was here before the Native American ... We had travelled here 3,000 – 50,000 years ago ... Yes you are right.. but at the end of the day.. "today".. this is the white man's house). We should move out of his house and get our own room at the YMCA or shelter, save our money and get an apartment, save our money and buy "our own" house and learn to take care of ourselves.

This way we both (Black America & white America) can be happy and Black America can grow up, become responsible for our own-selves and learn to love ourselves and take our rightful place on the world stage.

I think Malcolm was on to something.... May we should give it some thought?

In my opinion.

Tuesday, June 20, 2017

There are no days off from "believing in yourself"! None! You can't believe on Monday, Tuesday, Wednesday, Thursday, Friday, Saturday, Sunday, Monday, Tuesday, Wednesday, Thursday, Friday, Saturday, Sunday, Monday, Tuesday and then say "I'm going to take this Wednesday off from believing in myself" or "it's ok to not believe today".

Nah!! You can't never stop! This shit don't ever stop. If anything you gotta turn that shit up 2 more notches on the days when you don't feel it.

Saturday, May 06, 2017

Got a very important goal accomplished this past week. I filed my bankruptcy. Upon my discharge from bankruptcy, I'm freed up to really get involved in the entrepreneurial pursuits I love, most notably, real estate investing and options trading. It will be time to put down and execute my "Master Plan" that I mapped out and worked on in The Feds.
Now it's just a waiting game. I know how to do that.

HENRY WADSWORTH LONGFELLOW

"Be still, sad heart and cease repining
Behind the clouds is the sun still shining
Thy fate is the common fate of all
Into each life some rain must fall
Some days must be dark and dreary"

MELLE MEL -MELVIN GLOVER "BEAT STREET" - 1984

"A newspaper burns in the sand
And the headlines say man destroys man
Extra Extra read all the bad news
On the wall of peace that everybody would lose

The rise and fall that last great empire
The sound of the whole world caught on fire
The ruthless struggle the desperate gamble

That gain that left the whole world in shamble

The cheats, the lies and the alibies
And the foolish attempts to conquer the skies
Lost in space and what is it worth - huh
The president just forgot about Earth

Spending multi billions and maybe even trillions
The cost of weapons ran into zillions
There's gold in the street and there's diamonds under feet
And the children in Africa don't even eat

Flies on their faces, their living like mice
And their houses even make the ghetto look nice – huh
The water taste funny its forever to sunny
And they work all month and don't make no money

A fight for power, a nuclear shower
A people shout out in the darkest hour
The sights unseen, and voices unheard
And finally the bomb get the last word

Khrushchev killed (?) and German killed Jews
And everybody's bodies are used and abused – huh
Minds are poisoned and souls are polluted
Superiority complex is deep rooted

Elections and license and people got prices
Egomaniacs controlled the self-righteous
Nothing is sacred and nothing is pure
So the revelation of death is our cure

(?) Ceasar, Custard and Reagan
Napoleon, Castro, Mussolini and Begin
Genghis Khan and the Shah of Iran
Men spilled the blood of the weaker man

interchangeable
Dachau, Auschwitz, Hiroshima
A Vietnam, Leningrad, Iwo Jima
Okinawa, Korea, the Philippines
Devastation, death catch a killing machine

The peoples in terror, the leaders made an error
And now they can't even look in the mirror
Cause we gotta suffer while things get rougher
And that's the reason we got to get tougher

To learn from the past and work for the future
And don't be a slave to no computer
Cause the children of man inherits the land
And the future of the world is in your hands"

In my opinion, this is one of the all-time GREATEST Hip Hop versus every spoke into a microphone. Melle Mel said this shit back in 1984... if you look at CNN, MSNBC or Fox News today you can actually see this shit unfolding in real time. How prophetic! Thought provoking! Melle Mel has to be considered a seer and clairvoyant.

The fuckin' downside to this verse is that if you listen to "so called Hip Hop" of 2017... there is absolutely no MC today that is thinking along these lines or can fuck with the lyrical content of this verse! Not 1 MC!

On My Top 5 MC's in Hip Hop of all time:

1. Melle Mel – Furious 5
2. Chuck D – Public Enemy
3. Big Daddy Kane
4. Rakim
5. Brother J – X Clan

On My Top 5 "MC Voice's" in Hip Hop of all time

1. Kool Keith – Ultramagnetic MC's
2. Professor X – X Clan (This is protected by the Red, the Black and the Green)
3. Lakim Shabazz – Flavor Unit
4. Schoolly D
5. MCA – Beastie Boys

An Inside Job

To become what you desire to be, to be who you want to be, to attain whatever success you want, to rise above where you have been, to be better than who you were before, to face your fears, to face failure, to face and resist opposition, to overcome your weaknesses, to strengthen your strengths, to stop being worried, to cease being fearful, to cease being reckless, to stop being careless, to stop projecting negative outcomes, to start seeing victory, to begin to win, to begin to be strong, to be bold, to be assertive, to be confident, to be true, to be real, to be aggressive, to be a winner, to be a leader, to be an example by sight, to be whatever you can imagine or do anything that you want to do – I must first look inside of me and find it. It is right there. It has been always…it is now….and it always will be an INSIDE JOB!!

To My Sun Sean Xavier Gunby, Jr.

Sunday, July 2, 2017

I have to use my head for something more than a hat rack.

Monday, July 03, 2017

Most Black Americans I talk to regarding their upcoming or recent vacations always talk about Dominican Republic, Mexico, Jamaica, Bahamas, France or Europe. Hardly ever do I hear someone say "Yo…. I 'm on my way to Tanzania… or … I just came back from Angola and Uganda."…

I don't fuckin' understand this??? Hold up… Yes I do. 'Cause at one point I was the self-same Nigga. Thinking the Caribbean or Europe was the destination to be at. Until I went to Egypt (Egypt is on the continent of Africa) in 2008. I have since been to Egypt 3x, Sudan once, South Africa (Cape Town, Johannesburg, Durbin, Pumulanga, Kruger National Park) once and Swaziland once. My goal is to hit every country on the continent.

I've been to the Caribbean (Cuba, Jamaica, Bahamas), South America (Brazil), and North America (USA and Canada). To me, in my opinion, the continent of Africa is the most beautiful muthaphuckin' place I've ever seen. Yes, eventually I will get to Europe. I really want to go to Florence, Italy.

However, the Continent of Africa will always be my first destination of choice. I have received nothing but love and acceptance from the native African Bruthas, Sistas, cousins, uncles, aunts. Never once did I feel or experience any hostility from the native African people. Actually, they were happy to see me and welcomed me into their homes and huts.

Also, I felt more at home on the continent of Africa than I did here in New Jersey and I was born and raised here.

Black Americans need to muthaphuckin' rethink their vacation destinations. For the same amount of money you would spend going to Europe or the Caribbean ... you can spend the same amount of money or less and go the fuck HOME!

Raise your vibration and your mind up Niggaz and stop being a DUMB Nigga!!

Tuesday, July 04, 2017

I will not sit around and "hope", "wish", "dream" or "fantasize" about the life I want and not do the muthaphuckin' footwork! I gotta do the MUTHAPHUCKIN' FOOTWORK! It's as simple as that. There is no way around it.

I'mma will what the fuck it is that I want into existence. I'mma get up and make this shit happen! Watch me!

On Good White American People I've Encountered On My Journey:

As a Black American Male here in the United States of America, I have met, befriended and been cool with many white people along my journey.

Mr. J., (older white man of Polish heritage) was a member at the Upper Montclair CC in Clifton, New Jersey and owned and operated an Accountant Recruiting Placement Firm. After I caught my first felony in Atlanta, GA in 1992 – 93, I still completed my matriculation through Morris Brown College in Atlanta, GA and graduated with a BS Degree in Accounting. I came back to Jersey after college and went back to caddying at Upper Montclair Country Club where I had started caddying at 17 years old in 1986.

I was caddying for Mr. J. one day and the topic of my accounting degree came up and I told him about my case in Atlanta and the whole shit. He told me to call him that Monday and I did. Long story short...he placed me in the Accounts Receivable department at a company called HFS Incorporated located in Parsippany, New Jersey. This was October 1995. I stayed with that company for 3 years. Was promoted from Accounts Receivable to the Franchise Compliance Department (Legal), promoted again to Financial Analyst doing mergers & acquisitions of real estate brokerage firms nationwide. I materially participated in and was responsible for the acquisition numerous companies with Sales Volume in excess of $10 Billion Dollars.

Mr. J. took a chance on me and I didn't fuck him over and he helped me along my journey.

My man Dave F. I met this white dude in the 8th grade at Woodrow Wilson Jr. High School in Clifton, New Jersey. We hit it off immediately. Dave was one of those straight up white boys, wore a black leather motorcycle jacket from the 1980's, a Harley Davidson wallet with the chain, long straight hair down his back, listened to hard core Rock music and Heavy Metal shit. I mean a straight up white boy from the 1980's.

Here I was a Black kid fuckin' with RUN-DMC, Whodini, The Fat Boys, Hip Hop Music out! A break dancer wearing Lee twills jeans with the crease sown in the legs by the Chinese lady in Passaic next to Record City, name plate belt buckle, Puma Basket sneakers with fat laces (ironed every morning), afro with a Black Power pick in my back pocket with the Red, Black and Green fold down handle.

We stayed in touch over the years and played a lot of golf together. I told him about my Fed case so he knew what was up. When I got out the FEDS I called him and we started working out at his gym. He would get me in FREE with his pass.

One day I was broke as a muthaphucka 2 – 3 months out of prison, and I asked him for $100 to put in my pocket. Told him I didn't know when I could give it back to him. Dude didn't say one word. Dug in his pocket gave me a $100 and said "don't worry about it."

I paid him back a few months later.

Dave F. is a white dude that helped a Nigga out on his journey.

My man Joe (Italian Dude). I met Joe a while back in a 12 Step program we both attended. I remembered when that Nigga came walking in the meetings fucked up. I was there for him and helped him along to getting clean. We remained tight.

He knew about my Fed case and stayed in touch with me until I self-surrendered. When I got to prison I called him and asked him to put some money on my books/account. He asked me for my information and 2 days later I went on the computer and he had sent me $75.

I paid him back months after I got released.

Joe, a white dude, helped me on my journey.

As Nigga in America I have internal psychological conflicts. 'Cause it was white people (white America) that fucked my people around and continue to fuck us around to this day. Yet I've met many, many white people who were "aight" with me and treated me "aight".... I don't know what the fuck. But I had to include this in my book to keep this shit all the way real. I've come across a lot of fucked ass "crackaas" but I have also come across some good white people too. All white people ain't fucked up!

Word up!

On 77 Lake Ave, Clifton, New Jersey 07011:

My earliest recollection of life events and happenings takes me back to this address. An 8-unit apartment building in Clifton, NJ's, Botany Village" section. My mother and myself lived in "Apartment #8". Our telephone number was 546-5478. This was in the early to mid 1970's so you didn't have to have to dial the area code like you must in today's times.

The apartment was a 3 room apartment with a bathroom that had a stand-up shower and toilet and could not fit 2 people at the same time. There were 2 very small bed rooms with no closets. The room you entered in through the front door was the living room, eat in kitchen, card room, beer drinking room, shit talking room, stereo room, living room, family room, den, dining room. That muthaphucka was everything and there was always a lot of action going on in this room especially on Friday and Saturdays. There would usually be a couple of 6 packs of Rheingold on the table with Black women sitting down, smoking Kool or Winston cigarettes "talkin' shit".

This is around 1973 – 1978. The record player would have 7-8 records stacked on that silver piece in the middle that held the records up and would drop them automatically after the prior record played in it's entirety (45's or 33's). Aretha Franklin, Al Green, Stevie Wonder, The Jackson 5, Marvin Gaye, Sam Cooke, Jackie Wilson and Roberta Flack dominated the air waves in Apartment #8. We lived in the back of the building but you could hear the music in the front, back or side of the building.

These Black women, who all lived in various apartments within the building, would send me and my best friend at the time, Timothy Stevens, to Mr. Multz's drug store up the block at least 8x – 11x a day for packs of cigarettes or what have you. At that time, being that Mr. Multz (owner of the drugstore) new my mother and everyone in the building, he would give us the cigarettes no questions asked.

What's interesting about 77 Lake Ave, Clifton, NJ 07011, now that I look back on it is this. EVERY family/tenant in the building was Black American. All 8 units. Yet, at the time in the early 1970's, Clifton, New Jersey was a "lily white" town (I guessing 96% - 98%). I mean no Niggas, no Puerto Ricans, no Dominicans, no Arabs, no Asians of any kind, no nothing but white folks. That's it. Today in 2017, Clifton, NJ is a very diverse town with all sorts of ethnicities and nationalities. Not in the 1970's.

77 Lake Ave, all 8 families/tenants, was "1 big family", as a kid you could be chastised by adult in that building if your mother wasn't around and when your mother found out you was "actin' up" or "cuttin' a fool", you were sure to get your ass "toe up" in front of everybody. As kids, we had respect back then. Actually, the grown-ups DEMANDED that you were going to respect them! Period! All that fly talk, talking back, making faces or gestures when you didn't like what your mother said would get yo ass toe the fuck up! Then you had to go in the house and look out the window and watch all the other kids playing outside (this was worse than the whooping). But everybody, looked out for and helped each other in that building. If your mother needed a cup of sugar, a cup of milk, salt, pepper and paper towels, ANYTHING, ANYTHING, she would open the door and yell upstairs to Nancy or Vern and say "you got some sugar, milk?" and the answer would invariably always be "YES" and then she would send you (me) upstairs to get whatever it was she needed. That's how it was in that building during that time.

Also, one thing that shines through my mind very vividly about this time (1970's) and the families/tenants in my building in particular was that, everyone wore a "Black Power Afro" or "Natural". Every Nigga you seen on TV wore Black Power Afros. You saw them everywhere. Even Puerto Rican Niggas was wearing them back in the day. That was the shit. In my opinion, Black people were more "together" or "unified" back in the 1970's. I think this resulted from what our parents had lived and saw in the 1950's and especially the 1960's.

On Friday's and Saturdays... ahhhhhhhh man..., everybody's door was open and we went from apartment to apartment to apartment, outside, to the store, back inside, in the backyard, while the grown ups got drunk, start talking shit then start fighting!... lololololol (ohhhh shit.... Makes me laugh just writing about this shit). Everybody's stereo blasting Al Green, Stevie, Aretha, War, Marvin..... I loved this place. This building would be rocking "straight through" from Friday after work to Sunday morning. Then shit would get back to normal for the work week.

I remember my mother used to wash clothes in a washing machine hooked up to the sink with a rubber hose and that muthaphucka would vibrate during the spin cycle like it was getting ready to take off for flight. Then we had a "clothes line" that connected to our window with that "wheel and rope" that was connected to some pole or tree in the back yard and she would "hang out" the clothes to dry with "wooden clothes pins" and shit. Don't let it start raining while the clothes were on the clothes line then you would see Niggas hurrying up and "gittin them clothes in". Then when it stopped raining, they would hang them out again. As kids we used to run in between the clothes on the clothes line and shit. Pull them down, run into the bed sheets on the line.

Oh shit.... I remember the Mr. Softee ice cream truck would come and we would fuckin' go crazy telling our mothers to give us some change to get a ice cream cone. You get that muthaphucka and the ice cream be melting and shit running all down your arm on your clothes. But you didn't give a fuck... you had some ice cream.

My mother drove a Chevrolet Corvair and then she bought a white on white 1974 or 1976 Monte Carlo with the over/under headlights. She loved her Monte Carlo boy.. Damn!! "My Monte Carlo this" .. "My Monte Carlo that"... My mother was a Nurse's Aide at the time working at Daughters of Miriam nursing home on Hazel Street in Clifton. She later passed her New Jersey State Boards and became a Registered Nurse and still practices to this day.

On Growing Up In An All White Town and Matriculating Through An All White Public School System During the 1970's and 1980's:

I started going to Clifton, New Jersey Public Schools in around 1974. I started 1st grade at School #12 in Botany Village. The school was from 1st – 6th grades. Myself and Timmy Stephens were the only 2 Black kids in the entire school. I was in 1st grade and Timmy was in the 3rd grade. We both lived at 77 Lake Ave, Clifton.

In the 1st grade up to about the 6th grade I didn't even understand that I was different, was not aware of racial contrasts, race relations in the USA or racism. I don't think "any child" understands differences at that point. Kids at that age just want to play. All they want to do is play and they will play with any kid anywhere, anytime, any race, any creed, any religion, any size, etc., etc. They don't give a fuck about any of that shit. All they want to do is play.

I do remember vividly as if it were 7 minutes ago that my first day of school at School #12 my mother dropping me off and telling me

"if anybody put they hands on you or call you a Nigger...you got my permission to kick 'em in they ass"....

I was 5 years old maybe 6. I heard her loud and clear and followed those orders to a T.

You see, My Mother, was born and raised in rural Georgia in the 1940's and 1950's. She went to segregated schools in Lincolnton, GA and saw firsthand Jim Crow deep south racism. She saw the white kids in the white schools have better facilities, got better more up to date "latest & greatest" textbooks, more high school and college educated teachers, more concentrated learning environment and the list goes on.

In the Black segregated schools, from what was told to me by my mother, relatives on my fathers side and several different sources from other parts of the south during this time period of the 1940's – 1950's, Black children didn't go to school until maybe November because they had to work in the fields picking cotton, planting crops, raising animals and livestock and working on the family farm to help the family sell the crops and put food on the table.

My Grandfather "Papa" on my Father's side was a "sharecropper". This meant that he lived for FREE in a house owned by a white man on the white man's land. In exchange for this my Grandfather had to "work and till" the land by growing crops, animals, livestock, etc. Whatever my Grandfather produced would go to the white man for him to sell and they would split the proceeds (65/35) or something along these lines or whatever deal they worked out. The bigger share going to the white man.

The white man who owned the house and land owned a store and whatever Papa needed (soap, food, clothing, supplies, etc.) for his family, he would have to buy it from this white man's store on credit until the harvesting season was over and then they would "true it up" and settle the bill.

Well this meant that all of the children, especially the Black Male children had to work in the fields and on the farm EVERYDAY to help the family make it. So from what I've been told and I could be off some but I think I'm close, September and October are harvesting months (I think cotton is picked in October??) and EVERYBODY had to be working to harvest as much as possible to sell and store up food for the coming winter months. So there was no going to school for Black children until after this was taken care of.

So Black kids didn't go to school until November, after harvesting season, and had to stop going to school around March or April when Spring time came so that they could begin to plant crops and plow the land, etc. You must also take into consideration that the Black school teacher also had to juggle "teaching, farming and harvesting" at the same time. So most likely your teacher wasn't a high school graduate or college graduate.

From what I've been told by my father is that Papa ALWAYS owed the white man more than what he produced at the end of harvesting season and never got out of debt and this would cause him to go from farm-to-farm-farm-to-farm to take care of his family.

I have talked to several older Black men in the south and from the south during this time period and they have all concurred that "they had to work in the fields before school and after school" and some of them went no higher than the 5th, 7th, 8th, 9th grades before THEY HAD to work to help to support all their sisters, brothers, extended family and themselves. This was the Jim Crow south. The Deep South. Segregation in full effect.

So My Mother having lived through this and seen this shit firsthand, I guess she decided that Passaic Public Schools (majority Black) and Paterson Public Schools (majority Black) weren't going to do. I didn't understand it then but I do now. She saw that North Jersey was just as segregated as Georgia but was done with a "fake smile and handshake" as opposed to down south where white folks are "real" and will tell you straight out "we don't like Niggers and we don't want to integrate with Niggers".
I can respect a white Southerner more than I can a fake ass white Northerner. Cause that crakka in the south (not all) is a real muthaphucka and tells it like it is. Ain't no fakin'. He keepin' it 100! In no uncertain terms he lets you know where he stands. He is a man. I respect men who are men.

Conversely, the white Northerner, (not all), will "play like he cool with you", fake the funk like y'all alright and talk behind your back and work against you. Hate these types of muthaphuckas. Can't trust 'em.

My Mother wore a BIG Jackson 5 Black Power Afro, didn't take no shit and ALWAYS, ALWAYS, ALWAYS from the time I can remember, 4 – 5 years old, taught me and talked to me about Martin Luther King, Jr. (she called him Dr. King!), Malcom X, Angela Davis, the Black Panthers, the riots in Newark, NJ, Adam Clayton Powell and Black Power. She loved and respected Dr. King but she was more of a Malcolm X Nigga. She used to say to me with her southern accent straight out the Georgia woods, and I can remember it as if it were 4 minutes ago.

"Dr. King say…. If somebody slap you on your left cheek…you supposed to turn the other cheek and let them slap you on your right check"……. Malcolm X say… if you slap me I'mma kick yo ass!!…. I like Malcolm X…

You gotta git a education… Angela Davis had her PhD by the time she was 25… Adam Clayton Powell say "Burn Baby Burn"…

When they kill Dr. King… they riot in Newark… they had to call out the National Guard… if you was in Newark you couldn't get out…and if you was out you couldn't get in….

Always keep your head around you…. You gotta get an education.. you gotta get an education… "

I can safely say that over the course of my 48 years of life I've heard my mother say this to me at least 1,542 times.

I guess her sending me to school in Clifton, for her, she knew that I was getting the exact same information them white kids were getting and would not be "systematically left back" like Black kids in Passaic, Paterson or Newark, all school systems having been taken over by the State of New Jersey for poor scholastic test scores. I understand it now but I didn't back then.

I also guess that is why she made sure I knew I was Black and that I was proud to be Black.

I was always a gifted student academically. Very bright. In the 3rd grade (Ms. Grazioso) I was probably the top student in my class. I won the "Spelling Bee" and "Math Bee" every week. The winner would get a crown to signify his/her winning the contests. I kept the crown.

I think I remember hearing my mother or someone at School #12 saying that my IQ was around 129 in the 3rd grade. My mother loves to tell the story of how the Principal of the school at the time (Mr. Zarandonna), stopped her one day she was dropping off my house key to me so that I could get in the house after school.

From my mothers account, Mr. Zarandonna saw her in the office dropping off the key and approached her saying "are you Sean's or Timmy's mother? (she had to be there for us as we were the only 2 Blacks in the whole school).... And she said "yes, I'm Sean's mother". He then says to her "Do you know you have a genius?" and she said "Really???". And he went on to tell her how the other day he had went to Ms. Grazioso's class to observe her for evaluation and "happened to discreetly sit behind me".

My mother has always said that that was bullshit, that in fact he had went to observe this little Black boy killing shit, dominating his peers academically, which was me, as he had heard how bright I was.

He went on to tell her that Ms. Grazioso gave us a math test during his visit and that he saw me take my pencil and go "zip .. zip ..zip.. zip..zip..zip" and take my test and turn it in to the teacher before anyone else could finish their test. After observing me do this, that he thought to himself that it is impossible for this little Black boy to have finished his test so fast and in fact if he did, he couldn't have scored well. He then said to my mother "Ms. Gunby I went up and picked out Sean's test and you do know he had them all right?"...My mother was faking acting surprised said "Really?????"....She already knew what he just saw. He just couldn't believe seeing this little Black boy crushing shit like that on the academic tip. He then asked her incredulously..."Where did he learn that??".... and she said "Me!"..... lololololol

Little did he know that my mother used to drill me all the time at home with reading, writing and math going back to kindergarten. Academics has always come easy to The Black God, me. I could read and comprehend any muthphuckin' thing I desire. Anything. I have always been gifted this way. Math, numbers, writing, reading, understanding is a fuckin' piece of cake to me. Even to this day at 48 years old. I'm as sharp as a muthaphucka and can do anything I set my mind to. My issue back then was my behavior. Attention seeking, class clown, wanting to be down, wanting to be accepted by the wrong crowds, rebelliousness.

But all of my academic prowess would get dimmed once I started getting high smoking weed and drinking beer in the 7th grade. My behavior issues became magnified.

As I got older, 7th grade on up, Woodrow Wilson Jr. High School and Clifton High School, the differences between me and my white peers got pronounced. I stopped getting invited to parties my friends from 4th, 5th and 6th grade were now invited to. I didn't get invited to the Bar mitzvah of my Jewish friend and me and him were voted "Class Pals" in the 6th grade. His bar mitzvah was the next year in 7th grade.

I actually hated going to school in Clifton. I hated going to school with all those white kids.

White girls didn't find any interest in me (or were scared to publicly display same). Some did. You then look at the fact that you are Black and they are white. You are different. You go to Social Studies / History class and read the 3 paragraphs of how Blacks were savages from Africa, were made into slaves and were "saved" by the white man. This shit was being read aloud by the teacher in a class of 26 kids (25 white and 1 Black.. me)....lolololololol (ohhh shit... this shit is funny to me now but it hurt like a muthaphucka back in the 80's).

I saw white kids getting dropped off to school in Mercedes Benz's, BMW's and I had to walk, catch the bus or ride my bike to school. I started to get called "Nigger", "Porch Monkey", "Tar Baby", "Spear Chucker" on a regular basis now. Fighting most of the time when it happened but this didn't ease the inner gnawing, pain, and agony I felt about being constantly rejected, made to feel different and being different.

Teachers, coaches, administration all showing a condescension, contempt and slight for my presence.

When I was 12 – 13 years old and shit like this happens to me.. I internalized this shit and blamed myself. This was the beginning of my self-loathing, self-rejection and outright hatred of myself. In my opinion this also led to my drug addiction that almost killed my ass...

By the time I got to Clifton High School in 1985, which at the time was one of the biggest high schools in New Jersey, there were a few more Black kids but the school itself was still 98-99% white. I think there were close to 2,000 students in the entire school and maybe 10 Black kids. In my graduating class of 550 students there were 3 Black kids (2 females and me)..lolololololol ohh shit.

From my own experience and in my opinion, I don't think little Black Boys should go to a situation everyday during their most impressionable years where they face rejection, slights and mental/verbal harassment. In my opinion, little Black Boys in these years need to visibly see both Black male and Black females in positions of authority EVERYDAY. Children copy what they see.

I did meet some good solid white dudes and girls in Clifton High that were ok with me and treated me alright. I must say that.

Anyway, I persevered and made it through that shit, graduated "College Prep" and enrolled in Morris Brown College in Atlanta, Georgia in the Fall of 1987.

(a Historically Black College & University located in Atlanta, GA. Morris Brown College was at the time a member school of the Atlanta University Center comprising Morris Brown College, Clark College, Spelman College and Morehouse College. At that time, late 1980's, the Atlanta University Center was the largest institution for higher education for Black people on the planet earth. Morris Brown College was known as "The Black CPA Factory", as it graduated more Black Certified Public Accountants than any other private school of it's comparable size in the United States of America).

On The Dopest Hip Hop Producers of All Time (In My Opinion):

1. Marley Marl (Shante, Shan, G Rap, Kane)
2. Dr. Dre (Eazy E, NWA, Eminem, Snoop)
3. Mantronix (T La Rock, MC Tee, Just Ice, Joyce Sims)
4. KRS-ONE
5. Eric B
6. Kanye West

On Going Down South For the Summer as a Northern Black Kid During the 1970's and 1980's:

Starting at around age 6, every other year when school let out in Jersey in June, a week or so later I was on an Eastern Airlines flight from Newark, New Jersey to Augusta, Georgia, to spend the entire summer (June, July and August) "down souf" with my Mother's side of the family.

The next year or next summer I would go to Bennettsville, South Carolina and spend the entire summer "down souf" with my Fathers's side of the family.

On my Mother's side my Grandmother was called "Muh", she was the Matriarch of the house and law. I never met my Grandfather on my mother's side.

On my Father's side, my Grandfather was called "Papa" and my Grandmother was called "Mama". I have vague memories of both.

After this there were cousins, aunts, uncles, family and friends everywhere.

Down Souf was "way different" than Northern New Jersey mainly by how the people talked with that southern or "country" talk. We would say that "they talk country". Another thing that stood out upfront was the respect that children or "chaps" had for adults or "grown folks". When asked a question or told to do something, children would reply with "yes ma'am" or "ma'am" with no questions asked. Talking back or being disrespectful to any adult (family, friends) would get you fucked up or "a beatin". Beatin's were handed out with "switches", "broom sticks", "belts", "extension cords" or good ol' fashioned hands.

The houses both my Grandmothers had did not have the up to date bells and whistles like we had in our apartment up North or back in New Jersey. In Lincolnton, my uncle had to cut wood for us to have heat. My uncle Scoot, would cut a bunch of wood and we would carry that shit into the house and stack it behind "the stove". The "stove" was in the TV room where my Grandmother slept and that was the heat for the entire house. You had to keep feeding it wood and stirring it up to keep the heat going. You tried to sit or stand as close as you could to this stove to get warm.

My Grandmother had an "old kitchen" where she made and kept her own preserves or jelly, syrup and all types of shit that was truly organic. We had a bathroom with plumbing but we also had an "out house" where you went to take a shit or piss. It was detached and located outside of the main house across the road and you sat on a piece of wood to shit into the ground. It stank like a muthaphucka in there.

We also had a "smoke house" that had all types of shit in there like tools, bike parts, mini bikes, saws, all types of shit. We had chickens, pigs, horses, cows, rooster, hen, goats, dogs and cats. The rooster would be under the house right underneath where we slept and would crow every morning at the same exact time without fail.

We shucked corn, shelled peas and for the most part grew and prepared our own foods. Back then most people in the south had a garden where they grew their own tomatoes, corn, peas, collard greens, apple trees, pecan trees, muscadines, scupindines and all types of food. This was REAL ORGANIC shit 'cause you planted it, watered it, rain, harvested it, picked it, cleaned it, cooked it and ate it.

Back then the majority of people of all age groups were not super obese and fat like they are today. Most people were lean, trim, slim and vascular. You did not have all this diabetes, high blood pressure, cholesterol, anxiety and all this other bullshit you have in 2017. There must be a correlation to the food we consume now vs. back then.

When you got sick down souf, there was usually some "home remedy" that your aunt or Grandmother knew that would get you right without going to the emergency room, pharmacist or doctor. Some natural remedy shit that worked like clockwork.

Down souf, Blacks people and White people didn't interact too tough like they did in New Jersey. I remember when we would go "out town" I would hear about some stores we couldn't go in because "them white folks stores" or "that's the white folks restaurant". So it was definitely more defined down souf as to where Niggas were welcome and where they weren't welcome.

We would fish, hunt, walk in the woods and play all fuckin' day from the time we got up at 7-8 am until 9-10pm when we went to sleep. The clothes you put on in the morning where the clothes you wore all day. For breakfast you would eat grits, eggs, sausage or bacon and biscuits every morning. You would eat cereal with carnation milk in a can. For lunch we might eat a ketchup sandwich, mustard sandwich, mayonnaise sandwich or just some bread. Or you might pick a tomato out the garden and eat that muthaphucka. Soda's were real strong and good back then. You had to reach down into the soda cooler and get you a bottle soda and get the top off with a bottle opener. Coca Cola sodas back then were so strong that if you drank it too fast it would strangle you. We collected empty soda bottles and brought them back to the store for $.05 a piece. We would then use this money to buy candy.

The older Black men used to sit under the tree and play checkers all day and drink liquor and talk shit. The older the man was the less your chances were of beating him in a game of checkers. There were no red and black checkers. Instead bottle tops were used. One guy's bottle tops were "faced up" and the opponents bottle tops were "faced down".

I remember my Grandmother used to chew Bull Of The Wood tobacco and she had a spit can where she would spit out the tobacco juice. She would ask you to get her spit can for her if it was out of her reach. This can was the nastiest shit in the world to me and I hated when she asked me to get it for her.

We traced our roots back to something like "7 generations of Grandmothers" (I could be off here), to a Cherokee Native American Woman named "Emma Fox". She lived sometime around the 18th century (1790 something). We have a picture of her and it's amazing the resemblance of my Grandmother with this woman Emma Fox. We also had some white people in our family tree somewhere down the line. I don't know if it was by rape or mutual consenting adults??? I used to hear mother always talk about Hatchet Hogan a white man who was my Grandmothers brother or some shit like that.. I don't know exactly.

Going down souf to Lincolnton, Georgia was always an interesting experience for me being a kid from North Jersey.

Other summers I would go to Bennettsville, South Carolina and stay with my Aunt, her children and my cousins. My aunt had a pretty modern contemporary house for the 1970's – 1980's. It was brick with central AC, modern appliances with front and back yards. Man, I and we used to have some fun back in the day. We would walk to "Shady Rest" where my Grandmother on my father's side lived and that was an adventure in itself. Jumping the ditch, cutting through the bamboo forest, getting chased by dogs along the way and walking around all day in 90+ degree heat like it was nothing.

My grandmothers house wasn't as updated and modern as my aunt's and was ol' skool. We had work and chores to do everyday. Cut the grass, vacuum, wash the dishes, clean the house, sweep the driveway, clean the bathrooms and that house better be clean by the time my aunt got home or it was going to be some shit. But we always got the job done. These cousins of mine are more like brothers and sisters more than anything.

We would play all types of games and shit like "hide and go seek", "tag in the house", "hide the switch", "hitting with the belt", "UNO", "knuckles", "monopoly", "basketball outside in the dirt", "football", "throwing rocks at cars and trucks on the bypass", all types of shit ALL DAY LONG from the time we got up until the time we went to sleep. I loved going down there.

On The Most Influential Hip Hop Groups of All Time (In My Opinion):

7. Sugar Hill Gang
8. Furious 5
9. Treacherous 3
10. Fearless 4
11. Crash Crew
12. Sugar Hill Gang
13. RUN-DMC
14. Whodini
15. Fat Boys
16. Public Enemy
17. NWA

On The Black Male Cop In The United States of America:

In my opinion.....

I can't even imagine the psychological implications, mental and spiritual conflicts and mental anguish that must plague most Black Male cops. You work in a "job" that supports your rent/mortgage, food, shelter, clothing, child care, disposable income, etc. Everything that you own and will own going forward as long as you remain in this employ is tied to this "job".

Yet on this job, you see white cops engage in police brutality, display verbal contempt for Black people *(especially Black Men, a group of which you belong to first and foremost)*, spew racial epithets in private, public and they probably even show contempt and display an air of condescension toward you at the precinct while you both wear the uniform and off the job. And you can't say shit because your whole "economic life" is tied to this "job". You know some white cops who just flat out ain't shit and crooked as the letter S, yet you can't and won't say a fuckin' word.

When you are off the job in plain clothes......

You go to the mall or shopping and feel the "funny vibes" that come from all races of people who are just "straight up afraid of Black Men from the door". *(Not just white people, I get this from all races of people).* They don't know you are a cop as you are now NOT in uniform. You now you are just a Nigger like all of us.

You get pulled over by white cops while you are off duty and see and feel first-hand what the fuck it's like until you show your badge and let the white boy know "I'm on the job". Even then he looks at you suspiciously until he confirms same and doubts you still.

Black Brutha's and Real Niggas in the street don't fuck with you too tough cause they don't like police and we look at you like a Uncle Tom Coon Ass Nigga. Niggas look at you like an informant or traitor and ask themselves "How the fuck can this Nigga be a cop after Michael Brown, Trayvon Martin, Philando Castille, Sandra Bland, Eric Garner, Sean Bell, Laquan McDonald and the list goes on?".

So you don't get no love nowhere Black Cop. One minute you got all this power while you are in uniform then you clock out and you back to being an "expendable piece of shit Nigger" in America's eyes. This has got to fuck your head up. You get no love and no acceptance from nowhere.

Deep down you empathize with the Black Brutha on the street because your cousins, brother, uncle and father looks like him. He is you. You empathize with Sandra Bland cause your sister, cousins, aunt and mother looks like her. Yet you can't "be you" and "say what the fuck you want to say" cause your whole economic existence is tied up with this "job".

I would never want that balancing "act" you volunteered for. You can keep that shit.

On My Drug Addiction During The 1980's:

I will never forget it. Sometime around 1981. When it all started. A life experience that almost killed me but taught me so so much....as most of life's most challenging times do.

It was my 6th grade summer going into the 7th grade. A classmate of mine from 6th grade came to my house and told me he had 13 joints of weed and showed them to me. We went and immediately began to light them up. I didn't get high. It was either my first time ever, it was some bullshit weed or it was fake weed. Looking back on it now I think it was the latter.. fake weed. But shiiittt.....that didn't stop a Nigga from pursuing what he watched is Father do and couldn't wait to do for all those years. I had tried it so now I wasn't scared anymore.

Weed was and still is extremely easy to get so it wasn't too much time later that I was smoking weed and drinking beer on a regular weekend basis. By this time I was going into Woodrow Wilson Jr. High School in Clifton and it was a bunch of white boys up there selling weed and getting high before, during and after school. I loved getting high. I loved the way weed smelled. I loved smoking weed, drinking a couple of beers and getting fucked up with my friends at the time. That shit was fun. We would get fucked up and break (break dance).

Up to this point, 1981, before I started smoking weed I was an Awesome student academically (B average), All-Star short stop in Little League Baseball every year, played Little League Football, and basketball and all types of extra-curricular activities at the Clifton Boys Club were I excelled and dominated my peer group in damn near everything that went on at the Boys Club. All you got to do is ask any of the counselors who worked at the Boys Club in the 1980's about Sean Gunby and they will tell you. In 2011, I got voted into the Clifton Boys Club Hall of Fame. I always had behavioral issues in school but nothing too too bad. All of this was finna change in an instant.

Once I started getting high, my ambition, focus, drive and concentration for anything and everything was greatly diminished. I no longer wanted to go to practice for any sports and once it got too hard …. I quit. Just like a little pussy. I quit everything. My behavior got worse and worse and worse to now getting chased by cops, getting detention and suspended from school was all in motion. My relationship with my mother went downhill swiftly as my fucked up attitude now was out of control. And I didn't care.

Academics was never no sweat for The Black God (and still ain't), so I was always able to do just enough to pass and stay in "College Prep" classes and graduate high school and go to Morris Brown College.

I sniffed blow (cocaine) for the first time in the 11th grade, on my job where I pumped gas in around 1985. In the bathroom. I had bought some off this white dude at school and sniffed that shit that day. This began my "love hate" relationship with cocaine. I had seen my father and his boys sniff so shiiiiittttttt…… let me try that too. My cocaine addiction didn't really become a monster until I got to college around 1987. Up to this point, me and these white dudes I was hanging with were smoking weed, tripping of mescaline (LSD or tabs), smoking dust (PCP, Angel Dust), sniffing rush (I don't know what the fuck that was?), valiums, speed, drinking liquor, beer … all this shit and various times. At this point, I did not know it then but I was on the fast track of cold-blooded self-destruction and enjoying it.

I rebelled against any and everything. All I loved was Hip Hop! At this time RUN-DMC, Whodini, The Fat Boys, Grandmaster Flash and The Furious 5, Spoonie Gee, MC Shan, Mr. Magic's Rap Attack on Friday and Saturday nights, DJ Red Alert, Chuck Chillout, Treacherous 3, Fearless 4, Crash Crew, Kurtis Blow… all these Niggas was out with this new style, this new music that spoke to the youth of the 1980's, this attitude or rebellion, the clothes, the hats, the sneakers, gold rope chains, 92 KTU, 98.7 KISS, 107.5 WBLS, and they were Young Black Males like me and they had the entire Planet Earth captivated and hypnotized in a spell. I was one under this Hip Hop hypnosis and I loved them all. They spoke to me and I was going to listen and follow.

By this time, I'm no longer buying weed in Jersey. Fuck that, you got a better deal "going over", "goin' to the City" or going into New York City, more specifically…. Harlem USA. To me, when I go to NYC now it's like fuckin' Disney World, Six Flags type shit. New York in the 1980's was far far far from what it is today. By this time, the crack explosion, bomb, epidemic or crack plague was robust and pumping 8,000%. Graffiti covered the subway, buildings, walls, bodega pull down gates from top to bottom.. this personified NYC in the 1980's.

In the almanac, if you check the number of homicides and crime in NYC in 1988, 1989, 1990, it was something like around 1,900 homicides a year. It was a very dangerous place. That's like 5 muthaphuckas a day was getting killed in New York. The shit was truly a Wild, Wild West. But I gravitated to it, I enjoyed it and I loved "going over" to get high. The shit, the whole city, was grimy, dingy, reckless ..almost lawless. I loved going uptown to Harlem. On 145th & Edgecombe.. man you could get some fat ass pillow sacks of "nickels of weed" ($5 bag of weed). Good muthaphuckin' weed. As soon as you turned off 145th onto Edgecombe, niggas would bum rush your car on both sides selling you weed right out in the open.

Me being the Nigga that I was, I would go to Harlem and by 10 "nickels" and bring them back to Jersey and sell them for "dimes" ($10 bag of weed) to the white boys at school, the golf course and in the neighborhood. I had got so fly with them Niggas on 145th that I would go by 20 nickels and they would "kick me" (give for FREE) 4 or 5 extra nickels. So I had weed to smoke and sell and I kept money. By this time, I was caddying at the golf course making crazy money caddying and selling weed at the same time. I kept money.

Harlem USA, at this time, from my viewpoint, was HARLEM! There were no grey dudes (white boys), Asians (Chinese, Korean, India, Arabs) of any kind, Europeans and nobody else. Harlem was Black. From 170th street & Amsterdam down to 110th Street, Harlem was Big, Bold, Black and very Beautiful in it's Blackness. Dominicans had started to take over the west side from the George Washington Bridge on down to about 135th Street. Puerto Ricans "Spanish Harlem" was on the east side by 1st, 2nd Ave & 112th Street. But for the most part in the 1980's, Harlem was NIGGAZ! You could buy just about anything off 125th Street at that time. I loved hanging out in Harlem. Loved it.

New York City in the 1980's had a vibration that has long gone. Hip Hop was in it's purest form in the 1980's and NYC was the "Hip Hop Factory" pumping out Raw Hip Hop Shit every week on Mr. Magic's Rap Attack on 107.5 WBLS (Friday & Saturday nights from 9pm – 12am). You had DJ Red Alert & Chuck Chillout on 98.7 KISS (Friday & Saturday nights 9pm – 12am). I would go buy me a fresh Maxell, Memorex or TDK cassette tape on Friday during the day. By 8pm I was getting my shit ready. My box (radio), my tape (cassette), I used to have the "Record & Pause buttons pressed down ready for 9:01".

Yo, listening to the MasterMix on Friday and Saturday nights was fuckin' entertainment, for me, in my opinion. I mean, you was bound to hear some new shit that you didn't hear last week. Now at this time, Hip Hop is not played on the radio during the week at all, save a few of the Big Names (Melle Mel, Sugar Hill Gang, RUN-DMC, Whodini). At this time, the music industry was rebelling against Hip Hop music, art and culture. They said it was a fad that was going to die out. That it wasn't an art form. They called graffiti vandalism. I mean it was a fight for Hip Hop to survive and survive it did. Look at it now. MUTHAPHUCKIN' DOMINATION!

So when you made your tape on Friday & Saturday night, you listened to that muthaphucka all week until next Friday & Saturday. That was all the Hip Hop you were getting from the radio. No MTV, no satellite radio, youtube, internet, none of that shit. Mr. Magic, Marley Marl, DJ Red Alert, Chuck Chillout, The Awesome 2 (WHBI) **"held the keys"** to the Hip Hop Universe. Black Males, Black Men, from the Hip Hop Culture, living the Hip Hop Culture, pioneering the Hip Hop Culture, breathing the Hip Hop Culture, loving the Hip Hop Culture, who personified the Hip Hop Culture, contributors to the Hip Hop Culture….. **CONTROLLED HIP HOP CULTURE!** Not like today where you got some pussy ass white muthaphuckas who know nothing about the culture, don't identify with the culture making the decisions about the culture. This is why, In My Opinion, Hip Hop died sometime around 1990 or shortly thereafter.

I graduated from high school in June 1987. I had gotten accepted into Morris Brown College and was going to Atlanta, Georgia in August 1987 for the Fall Semester. That summer, 1987, my addiction really took off. I was sniffing coke all the time. I loved cocaine. I loved sniffing blow. I loved getting "skeed". I would get "skeed" and start talking out of my fucking head about all types of shit and topics. I loved getting the "drips" and my whole entire face being numbed the fuck out. We used to "go over" on the bus to Port Authority, jump on the A or AA train uptown to 163rd & St. Nicholas Avenue, cop some blow from the Spanish dudes standing in front of the bodedga, then walk up to 164th & Amsterdam and cop an ounce or 2 of weed, buy a Ballantine Ale or Schlitz Malt Liquor Bull (sip that shit through a straw), walk down to 155th & St. Nicholas and sit in the park overlooking The Bronx and Yankee Stadium and get fucked up. Then we would jump on the train at 155th, back to Port Authority then back to Jersey.

By this time, grams of blow in NYC were going for $25 - $40 a gram. I remember I started off just buying "half a gram" and that would last me all night. By the time I got ready to go to college, I was buying an "8 Ball" (3 ½ grams) for myself for the night. I was fuckin' out of control. But I always knew I was leaving Jersey/NYC and going to Atlanta, where in my mind I thought I would be 856 miles from Harlem and safe. WRONG!!!!!!

What I didn't know at the time but would later learn is that **"Wherever you go you take you with you!"**.

I got to Morris Brown College in Atlanta, Georgia in August 1987. My mother dropped me off at Borders Towers, Room #306. We went to The West End to a First Atlanta Bank, she deposited $400 into a checking account for me, got me a Tillie Card and told me "I'll see you later" and she got back on I-85 North headed back to New Jersey. And there I was, 18 years old, 856 miles away from North Jersey, on my own and I didn't even know how to wash clothes. All I knew were the buzz words "detergent" and "bleach" but had no fuckin' idea of what to do with either of them.

My mother getting me out of New Jersey and "dropping me off" in Atlanta, GA, for me to fend for myself was another "pivot moment" in my life and one of the best educational lessons she has ever taught me. I got home sick around October and me and another brother from Paterson, New Jersey drove to Jersey to cure our "home sickness". I went home for Thanksgiving and when the 1st semester was over in December, I went home for Christmas break. After being in Jersey for 96 hours during Christmas break, I missed Atlanta and I missed being on my own. Having been away from my mother and on my own for 120 days, I "grew" and "knew" that I could make it, that I could take care of myself and I never went back to live with my mother again since.

These Black Mothers today are the main culprits in "pussyfying" these young Black Boys. They take care of them, take care of them, take care of them, take care of them, take care of them, take care of them, from 6 months old until 30 years old these able-bodied muthaphuckas are still living at home with mom with her titty in their mouths and they are utterly USELESS!

Sorry for my digression. Let's get back to my drug addiction.

Getting to Atlanta and into college was at the time, I thought erroneously, a safe-haven, a fresh start for me and that my addiction was over. Up to this point, I was convinced that the George Washington Bridge, Washington Heights, Harlem, 163rd Street, 138th Street, 141st Street was my problem and that if I just got far, far far away from NYC I would be ok. WRONG!!
"Wherever you go you take you with you!"

Immediately on campus Niggas was getting drunk and smoking weed. Shiiiiitt. I willingly under my own volition, participated. I found all of the weed spots in and around the AUC (Atlanta University Center). The first 3 semesters I was cum laude honor roll student with a GPA of 3.0 or better. I did this and I smoked at least a dime bag of weed and drank a 40oz of Mickeys, Old English 800 or Schlitz Malt Liquor Bull EVERYDAY. A Nigga was getting fucked up every day and still making the honor roll. I thought to myself "I don't have a problem". A Nigga is just gifted like that. When you are a superior being you can do shit like that!

Whenever I would go back to Jersey for Christmas break, Spring Break or summer break I would sniff blow. I remember around the Summer of 1989 while caddying at the golf course, I was getting so fucked up sniffing cocaine that me and my man (whose name I won't mention), would caddy all day 36 – 45 holes, leave the golf course, go to Harlem, sniff cocaine all night until 7am, go back to Jersey and go straight to the golf course, caddy all day 36 holes, leave the golf course, go to Harlem, sniff blow all night until 7am, go straight to the golf course and caddy all day again 36 holes. No sleep and very little food. The shit was insane now that I think about it. I was sniffing out on the golf course while I was caddying for my group. My nose use to bleed like crazy.

One of the caddies that used to get high too, saw my nose bleeding and said to me "if you smoke it your nose won't bleed no more"... lololololo ohhhh shit...olololololololol WOW! This shit is hilarious to me now. I took his suggestion and started smoking crack with a stem. This was the beginning of the end. Within 6 months the wheels came off and I was fuckin' out of control. I had lost mad stupid weight, I was unemployable, I couldn't keep a job, I had dropped out of Morris Brown College and I was ALL THE WAY FUCKED UP! Bankhead Courts, Perry Homes, Dixie Hill, McDaniel Glen, Ashby Street had become my stomping grounds. I had destroyed myself. Dignity, self-esteem, motivation, energy, focus, determination, drive, enthusiasm, appetite, sleep, confidence, belief, faith in myself, I had none of....all on ZERO!

What I replaced them with was shame, regret, remorse, humiliation, self-hatred, fear, loneliness, embarrassment, self-rejection, degradation, self-abnegation, self-loathing, hurt, pain, anger, mental anguish, physical malnutrition... ALL THIS SHIT I FELT AT THE SAME MUTHAPHUCKIN' TIME.... I was broken to the core.

I called a lady friend of mine at the time and told her **"call somebody .. I need to go get some help"**.. She did and this brutha named, Nate Mack, came to pick me up at my apartment in Austell, Georgia on October 15, 1990, and he took me to a treatment center in Smyrna, Georgia called Brawner Psychiatric Institute. The treatment program housed there was named COALESCE. My counselor was a lady named Stephanie and she helped a Nigga immensely. I haven't had a drink or a drug since that day. As of the writing of this page, I have been clean for 26 years, 10 months and 32 days... in-a-row Niggas! No relapse.

I'mma Bad Muthaphucka!

On Wells Fargo Bank Fraud "Fake Account Scandal... 2013 – 2017":

Senator Elizabeth Warren (D – Massachusetts) thank you for your courage. It is refreshing to watch the videos of you standing up and saying what the fuck it is you have to say. I love that. I respect that.

My following synopsis on the Wells Fargo Fake Account Scandal is cursory and may contain some mistakes, however, none of my synopsis will be deliberately intentional to mislead or misspeak.

From about 2013, as far as we know, up until 2017 (48 months or 4 years), Wells Fargo Bank engaged in unilaterally, under it's own volition, "creating fake accounts" for current Wells Fargo customers for shit they didn't need or ask for. Wells Fargo would bill these customers and direct debit or add fees and charges on to monthly statements for services customers didn't ask for. The setting up of these accounts were deliberate, premeditated and knowingly false from the outset.

Wells Fargo's stock price appreciated and soared as a result of the then Chairman of the Board and CEO, John Stumpf, touting how great the company was doing operationally and all the profits that were being generated as a result of "cross selling accounts" to customers. His goal was to have each Wells Fargo customer have at least 6 – 8 different accounts with the bank. He would go on earnings calls every quarter and tell Wall Street analysts how great the bank was doing with cross selling to it's existing customer base. Wall Street ate it up and the stock price soared. The CEO owned about 6,000,000 shares of Wells Fargo common stock. His "personal" paper profits soared with the stock price.

They spun the story that this all happened as a result of "lower level management and employees" conspired to execute this plan. Over 5,300 people were fired or lost their jobs as a result. This is some straight bullshit! A woman (Tolstead??)who reported directly to the CEO oversaw all of this nonsense. She resigned from the bank with a $125,000,000 "Golden Parachute" retirement package and has faded into the ether. John Stumpf stepped down and appeared before Senate Hearings addressing this fraud. He showed up with a cast on his hand and proceeded to expound upon how these lower level employees only made up a fraction of the total Wells Fargo labor force. Elizabeth Warren (D – Massachusetts) ripped that Nigga live on video, made him look like a little boy.

As you know, I have a BS in Accounting from Morris Brown College, Atlanta, GA and a MS in Financial Management from the New Jersey Institute of Technology, Newark, NJ.

What we learned is that in a publicly traded company, anyone with a title of Vice President or higher is considered an "officer of the company" and can bind the company, bank or firm legally with his/her signature (may vary from firm to firm depending upon the charter, bylaws, etc.). This means that anything that happens in that company, bank or firm that fucked up, negligent or fraudulent is the responsibility of the Board of Directors, Chairman and CEO, and anyone else who knowingly participated in the fraud. A California judge ordered Wells Fargo to pay $142,000,000 in a class-action settlement.

What happened at Wells Fargo was fraudulent, there were accounting irregularities, financial statement misstatements, "cooked books", insider trading and the list goes on. ALL INTENTIONAL! ALL DELIBERATE! From what I see, nobody was indicted by the United States Department of Justice or Securities and Exchange Commission. Why? Why was nobody criminally charged? This is some straight bullshit. Sean X. Gunby, Sr. goes to federal prison for 16 months for $84,000, and I have to pay that back as my restitution which ballooned to $106,000 as soon as I stepped foot out of FCI Morgantown. They took $25 a month off my books every month I was in the joint when I made $5.12 per month as a Window Washer and $32 a month working in the Education Department. I should have gone to prison as a result of my disregard and open and notorious violation of the US Tax Code when I was raised better, trained better and knew better. I blame nobody but me for this.

Somebody is not playing right? The United States of America is not playing fair. The Department of Justice is showing that it is selective in it's prosecutions. The Securities and Exchange Commission is not playing right. Somebody cheatin'! Some straight weak nigga sucka shit. I been knew this but had to highlight same. I understand that I don't have the "complexion for the protection". The Art of War by Sun Tzu says that to keep order and discipline in a just society, "everybody high and low should be treated alike".

When you commit a "federal white collar crime" your sentenced is based of the "amount of money" that was fucked up and "the number of people affected" by the crime. That number is then used to determine your points and where you fall on the US Sentencing Guidelines Chart. The amount of money that was fucked up from 2013 – 2017 by the Board of Directors and all the characters involved would have put all of them muthaphuckas Category I probably Level 30 or better and them niggas would have been looking at "20 balls" at a minimum or "30 balls" or better. That's 240 months (20 years), 360 months (30 years). And you can't go to no "minimum security" or "low" with that kind of sentence.

You start off at them USP's, Medium Highs where you gotta take showers with your boots on and get your homeboy to watch out for you to take a nap when them doors open (stories I was told by Niggas that's been up there) until you work your way down to under 10 years to get to a "low". And at them USP's and Medium Highs, when they have the "paperwork party" your paperwork can't be fucked up.. No 5K1's or Safety Valves allowed up there. They ain't goin' for it! That's where they would have went and should have went.

It's ok though... The Sun, Moon and Stars "sees everything" and what you put out into The Universe always comes back to you even though it may not be witnessed by others.

Peace Out!

Made in the USA
Middletown, DE
31 March 2021